Lessons from the Obstacle Course

Five Strategies to Conquer the Muddy Fields of Life

Kelly Majdan

Lessons from the Obstacle Course © 2022 by Kelly Majdan.
All rights reserved.

Published by Ethos Collective

All rights reserved. This book contains material protected under international and federal copyright laws and treaties. Any unauthorized reprint or use of this material is prohibited. No part of this book may be reproduced or transmitted in any form or by any means, electronic or mechanical, including photocopying, recording, or by any information storage and retrieval system, without express written permission from the author.

Identifiers:
LCCN: 2023903721
ISBN: 978-1-63680-122-3 (paperback)
ISBN: 978-1-63680-123-0 (hardback)
ISBN: 978-1-63680-124-7 (ebook)

Available in paperback, hardback, e-book, and audiobook

Any Internet addresses (websites, blogs, etc.) and telephone numbers printed in this book are offered as a resource. They are not intended in any way to be or imply an endorsement by Ethos Collective, nor does Ethos Collective vouch for the content of these sites and numbers for the life of this book.

Lessons from the Obstacle Course

This book is dedicated to my husband, Frank, for always being my *Rock* and biggest fan.

To our kids, Gavin and Tori, you two impress and inspire me to be the best I can be.

To all those who put together these crazy obstacle course races to create challenging yet fun events. I have learned so much and am forever grateful.

&

To the many race participants who we have met along the way for the great conversations, the inspiration and support, and the family environment you embody.

Thank you!

CONTENTS

A Note to You–the Reader............................ ix
Origin Story xiii

PART 1—RECOVERY

Chapter 1:   The Bull Pen........................3
Chapter 2:   Tarzan Swing......................15
Chapter 3:   Gauntlet 2.0......................23

PART 2—DISCOVERY

Chapter 4:   The Continental Divide..............39
Chapter 5:   Pegatron 53
Chapter 6:   The Sewer and Up from the Grave.......61

PART 3—PERSISTENCY

Chapter 7:   Conquerors Carry 71
Chapter 8:   Rockies 81
Chapter 9:   Board Crawl 91

PART 4—CREATIVITY

Chapter 10: Walking the Tightrope...............103
Chapter 11: Walk the Plank 111
Chapter 12: Virtual Races.....................119

Part 5—Collaboration

Chapter 13: Boardwalk........................135
Chapter 14: Walls of Fury....................143
Chapter 15: Tiger Trap, Great Wall of America,
              and More 151

Finale—After the Race

Chapter 16: The Bling 167

Acknowledgments..............................175
Endnotes.....................................179

A NOTE TO YOU—THE READER

According to Cambridge Dictionary, the definition of an obstacle is *something that blocks you so that movement, going forward, or action is prevented or made more difficult.* In obstacle course races (OCR), the intention of having an obstacle in your path is for you to find a way to overcome the challenge presented. That is the goal of these races, to see how many of these obstacles you can overcome, with or without assistance. And for those in the competitive round, to see how fast you can do so.

What is interesting is that we face more obstacles in life than we do on the course. However, we do not seem to understand that these challenges are meant to be in our path, like they are in an OCR, so that we can find a way to overcome them and learn from them. Instead, we succumb to them, we let them ruin our day, or we get annoyed that they are even there in the first place.

What would happen if you approached life's obstacles the way you did when you encountered them on the course? With the determination that you will take them on as best you can or drop to do your burpees so you can move forward to take on the next one? Vowing to try harder the next time you encounter them or being satisfied that you did your best and enjoyed the experience?

We all know that life is not meant to be easy. We will face challenges. We will encounter adversity, and we will occasionally struggle. But that is part of what life is all about and what makes us each stronger, better human beings. Each challenge provides us with an opportunity to test our mental fortitude, to see how creative we can get, and to find our purpose deep inside to take on the challenge, regardless of whether or not we will succeed.

Sometimes the struggle will get long, we will get tired, and we will feel like the challenges will never end. But just like a long race, eventually, they do. Eventually, you cross the finish line of a long trial and are rewarded with the knowledge that you faced your challenges, your demons, your doubts, your adversaries and you prevailed.

The great Stoic, Marcus Aurelius, wrote, *"Our actions may be impeded, but there can be no impeding our intentions or dispositions. Because we can accommodate and adapt."* These obstacle course races teach us many things about how to adapt and overcome. How to reach down deep and find our strength to make it through the challenge in front of us. And if you are paying attention to what you are feeling and thinking on these courses, you will find the lessons that will teach you how to adapt and overcome the obstacles you face in life.

In the pages that follow, you will not find detailed instructions, tactics, or tips on how to physically take on some of the challenges in these obstacle course races. Instead, this book is about tackling your mind, your fears, and all the other things that might prevent you from achieving your goals. The backdrop is the obstacles on the course. The outcome is using these strategies and lessons to take on the obstacles in life.

It is also about regaining your power by taking control of how you react to obstacles in your path, unexpected events in your life, and your negative mental chatter. Using the observations of my reactions to the challenges on these courses, I will discuss how these are similar to the feelings we have when we encounter challenges in life. The strategies used to overcome them on the course are the same ones you can deploy to take on obstacles in life.

LESSONS FROM THE OBSTACLE COURSE

We will discuss a little about parenting, aging, business, finances, teamwork, and health. At the end of each chapter, I will recap the lessons from the strategy we discussed and provide an action plan with some questions to help you dig deeper, hopefully leading to some personal insights into a challenge you might have.

I wrote this because I am an ordinary person, just like you. We have had a few medical scares and some physical challenges to overcome; I imagine like you in some way. I am a mother, a wife, a friend, and a small business owner. I am just an ordinary person trying to make ends meet every day. We didn't have a huge issue to overcome in our lives, quite the contrary, and that is the point. We don't need to have huge obstacles in our lives to trip us up—the small ones can do that just fine. It is how we face them and overcome them that makes all the difference in where we end up in life.

For those of you who have participated in these challenges, maybe you might find that you had similar experiences during these races. That you had some of the same thoughts and used some of the same strategies on the course. Whatever the case may be, I hope you will find some inspiration in these pages to take on the hard things in life. To not give up or give in. To look for more out of your life and to play fully. Maybe you might even be inspired to take on an obstacle course if you haven't done so. Or take on another one if you have but with a different mindset than you had before.

We all know that life will present us with challenges and obstacles to overcome; that is a big part of what life is all about. Choose to take them on with the joy and fun you have on race day, ready to see how many you can overcome and to celebrate the day knowing you showed up and did your best.

To living life fully!

~Kelly Majdan

ORIGIN STORY

Where does your story begin?

A hero is an ordinary individual who has found a better way to mask their human frailties.

—Superman, *Superman*

"Honey, take the keys. You need to drive home tonight." My husband, Frank, said this as we were leaving his parents' house one night in the spring of 2013. This was odd for him to ask because he doesn't like to give up control of the driver's seat. My husband and I like to give each other a hard time about who is the better driver. You might say we compete on this topic. For him to hand over the keys was rather strange. We had been at his parents' house in Bella Vista, Arkansas, the drive home was windy, and it was darker than usual that night. He had not been drinking, so I found it odd for him to ask me to drive. He said he had a headache and could not focus on the road. So, I took the keys and drove us all home. But now, I had some questions for him.

Throughout the past few years, I had noticed my husband wasn't as much fun as he used to be. Sometimes, he was downright cranky. We enjoyed things like roller coaster rides, hiking, biking, running, and most physical activities.

Now that the kids were getting older and we could do more of these adventures as a family, we tried to do them as often as possible, given all the kids' other commitments. But more and more, my husband got tired faster, complained of headaches, or both. That night, when he asked me to drive, I knew something more than being overworked, getting older, and raising a family was going on. So, when we got home, we had what all couples who are working through an issue have—a good old-fashioned heart-to-heart talk.

"So, what's going on?" I asked.

"Nothing. Well, nothing, really. I'm just seeing double."

"Double? What do you mean double?"

"Well, I see two of you stacked on top of each other."

"How long has this been going on?"

"Oh, I don't know, maybe since we moved here."

"WHAT? We moved here five years ago, and you are just now telling me?"

Getting my husband to see a doctor is close to impossible. Maybe you can relate to this, or maybe this is only a Marine or man thing, or maybe both. I mean, a bone must be protruding from his leg and blood squirting everywhere before he would admit that he is injured in any sort of way, much less so much so that he needs to see a doctor. So, after our heart-to-heart discussion, when I suggested he go to a doctor because seeing double is not normal, his response did not surprise me.

"It's not that bad," he said.

"Really? Not that bad? You are telling me you cannot drive home safely because seeing double makes it hard to stay on the road at night, and it is not that bad? Honey, that is not normal!"

At this time, our son was seeing a specialist for eye therapy, and I nagged my husband into scheduling an examination with him to find out why he had double vision. After the appointment, my husband came home and proudly stated he only needed prism eyeglasses, and he was more than happy to pronounce the problem solved!

"Great," I said. Then I asked what most husbands don't want to be asked when they believe they have solved a problem. "Did you ask him *why* you need to wear prism eyeglasses?"

"Uh, no." He had this sheepish look on his face, like he just got caught with his hand in the cookie jar.

Geeze!! Really, honey? Now I am not a BAND-AID®-type person. If you tell me I must apply the bandage, I will. But I want to know why and whether it is all I need to help me heal. Those prism eyeglasses were a bandage. Double vision is not normal, and I couldn't believe that those glasses would fix the underlying problem. So, I kept hounding him to get a second opinion.

We proceeded like this for a few more months until our son ran his eye into the back of an arrow's feathered end as he chased his sister and tried to shoot her with it. Now, before you think of us as terrible parents, let me explain. The arrow was a suction-cup arrow, and it got stuck on my daughter's door as she slammed it while running from her brother. He forgot to stop when the door came to an abrupt close, which meant he ran into the back part of the arrow. We are thankful that he only ended up with a cut to the white of his eye, but this little incident put us in touch with a great optometrist in our area. And I convinced my husband to get a second opinion about why he was seeing double.

The optometrist referred us to a neurologist, who sent my husband to get an MRI, and at last, we discovered the potential cause of Frank's double vision on January 21, 2014. My husband had a pineal gland cystic mass, 16.2 mm x 16.2 mm x 11.6 mm, sitting in the middle of his brain. We felt we finally had our answer, but now we had to fix the problem. This sent us off to a wonderful neurosurgeon at UAMS in

Little Rock, Arkansas, who, after only a five-minute visit with us, told his assistant to schedule Frank for surgery as soon as possible. I stopped the doctor because I knew my husband wasn't going to and asked him the same question I had asked before. "Why?" Brain surgery might be an everyday thing for him, but not for us! He showed us a normal brain MRI, then Frank's. Sure enough, there was a blob in the middle of his brain, which the kind doctor pointed to and said, "That should not be there." Okay, now I understand!

The next few months were a blur. I went into must-get-things-done survival mode to get everything prepared for his surgery and the months of recovery afterward. Frank had his brain surgery on March 12, 2014. After almost 4 hours of surgery, the doctor proclaimed victory—he had successfully removed the entire cyst from my husband's brain. I would later tell Frank's sisters that not only did the good doctor get the entire cyst out, but after all these years, it would please them to know that their brother really did have a brain!

THE INTRODUCTION

As Frank recovered from surgery, a wonderful group of work friends invited me to join them in a race called the Warrior Dash. I had no idea what it was, but in my usual style of jumping right in when someone asked me to do something that sounded like fun, I said yes. You might have this same tendency—the one that gets you into a bit of trouble sometimes because you leap before you think. But it can also open a lot of great opportunities and experiences for you too. This race would be the latter of the two.

In May of 2014, we all caravanned to this dirty field on the outskirts of Tulsa, Oklahoma, to participate in this very muddy obstacle course race (OCR). My husband could not participate in this one because he was still recovering from brain surgery, after all. But watching all of us have fun on the course planted the seed that would help motivate him to focus on his recovery so he could participate in an OCR in the fall of 2015.

Like many beginnings, we didn't know then that this was the start of what has now become our crazy obstacle course race journey. Over the next eight years and many obstacle course races, we have discovered that the mental fortitude we needed to get through many of those course challenges was the same mental grit and determination we used to get through many obstacles we have encountered in life and business.

ORIGIN STORIES

Every one of us has an origin story. This is not a unique thing that Marvel or DC or any other superhero movie invented. We all started from somewhere, and something in our lives has influenced us, defined who we are, and shaped our perceptions. We all have experiences from birth through our childhood, adolescence, and onward that set us on the path to who we are now or changed us from who we were to who we are meant to be.

Growing up in the 70s and 80s, my heroes were Wonder Woman and Princess Leia. I always thought it would be so cool to fight off any danger with strength, smarts, and those awesome bracelets! Whenever we played as kids, those two were my go-to characters. It also helped that while growing up, I had mostly guy friends, so I didn't have to fight for the coveted female spot in our make-believe universe.

My husband's favorite go-to character was always Captain America. His mother likes to share that when he was younger, to get him dressed for church, he had to wear his Captain America belt buckle. She still has a great picture of him wearing that belt buckle! So, it didn't surprise me much that after college, he attended the Officer Candidate School for the United States Marine Corps. To this day, that superhero persona suits him very well!

As you get older, though, and start logging more life miles behind you, that magical superhero persona can fade away as you work hard to be the adult in the room raising kids, fighting for promotions, starting a business, or starting over again in any area of your life. The fun seems to fade, and life trudges on. This is how it seemed to me as we moved through our forties, raising kids, building our careers, starting a business, and trying to balance it all as the aging process and life in general started to show signs of wear and tear in our health, our bodies, and our moods. Then Frank had brain surgery, and the reality that we were just trudging along in life and going through the motions hit home and hit home hard!

Whether you acknowledge it or not, when times get challenging, you can still reach inside to pull out that superhero persona you leaned on as a kid. Call it your internal strength or your make-believe universe; it's that thing that makes it easier to get through the situation at hand. We all have a superhero inside us that propels us through some of our toughest times in life. As you get older, though, tapping into this inner strength can get more difficult, causing you to give up on the challenge at hand, which means you are giving up on yourself.

Finding that inner superhero, or strength, will not only help you manage the challenges you face in life, but it will also help you to define how you will overcome them and prevail. So what is your origin story? Who did you admire when you were growing up? What traits did you like? What was it about this person or superhero that made you want to be like them? What characteristics can you lean into when times get tough?

When you sense that the road ahead will be challenging, learning to re-ignite this inner persona will help you take on the obstacles in your path and come out triumphant on the other side. The following chapters will give you ideas and questions to help you tap into your hidden strengths to triumphantly take on any challenge you may face in life.

The Five Strategies

In this book, I share the life lessons and strategies we discovered on those muddy obstacle courses. Each obstacle you encounter in these races teaches you something about yourself that you can use to take on the many obstacles you encounter off the course. In the chapters that follow, I will explain five strategies we leaned on when completing those muddy courses and show you how you can use those same strategies to get through the obstacles you face in life.

These strategies might not be in the order of how you may encounter them, and many times you will use a strategy more than once. However, recognizing and being able to use these strategies will give you the mental fortitude you might need to propel you to victory over the evil villains, or obstacles, you encounter in life.

Often, the first strategy you must deploy is Recovery. This is when you acknowledge a hurt or an injury that is holding you back. Where you work through why it is preventing you from moving forward and identify any goals that will encourage you to move past the obstacle. In Discovery, you will uncover your purpose and why you feel compelled to overcome the obstacles in your path. You will also decide which ones you should avoid and not take on and learn to be okay with that. Through Persistency, you muster the mental fortitude to keep up the good fight, even when the odds are stacked against you, or you are too tired to continue. Some obstacles will force you to find your inner Creativity to discover new ways to fight the battle, overcome the challenges, and forge ahead. And through Collaboration, you acknowledge, as the Avengers and Justice League superheroes did, that some obstacles are too big or challenging to fight on your own. You accept your need for others' assistance and that they need you to overcome and complete the obstacle in front of you. These OCRs have great life lessons that we all can learn from and use to forge ahead and become stronger than we ever thought we could be as we take on the obstacles that life places before us.

So are you ready to test your resolve?
Are you ready to get muddy?
Then let's head to the starting line!

PART 1
RECOVERY

1

THE BULL PEN

WHAT MOTIVATES YOU?

I choose to run towards my problems and not away from them.
Because that's what heroes do.

—Thor, *Thor Ragnarok*

The first obstacle course race (OCR) we attempted together was called Conquer the Gauntlet™. According to their website www.conquerthegauntlet.com (feel free to read this in that deep announcer voice), "Conquer the Gauntlet is the most EXTREME 4 miles on the planet. Race through grueling terrain and CONQUER over 25 of the largest, most unique, and challenging obstacles on Earth!"[1] Now, to some, this might sound daunting, but to us, it sounded like the challenge we were looking for. We were all in and wanted this to be the capstone for Frank's brain-surgery recovery. Plus, I had so much fun on the first one, we were looking forward to taking on something different and challenging. These races fit this desire perfectly.

Before we signed up, though, I wanted to make sure Frank got a clean bill of health and the okay from his doctor. At this early point in our journey, we knew very little about obstacle course races in general and didn't want to travel too far. So, we chose a race that was close to home and would give Frank enough time to recover. The race took place in Little Rock, Arkansas in September 2015, which was about a year and a half after his surgery. According to my husband, though, it was too far out on the calendar. He wanted to go now. But we both knew he needed time to recover and regain his strength. So, I stretched out the date as far as I could and insisted we get his doctor's all-clear first.

The recovery process

Frank worked hard to get back into shape after lying in bed for a few months. We had a few challenges with his recovery, which stretched out his bed-rest time. As soon as the doctor cleared him to get off bed rest, he wanted to jump right back into physical training. My first attempt to get him back into shape was with yoga and some stretching. Well, the poor guy dislocated his hip during one of our yoga sessions—yes, doing yoga! I figure that is what happens when a Marine does yoga; he decided a little stretch was not enough, that he could and should push a little further. A more pain, more gain attitude was not exactly what the doctor ordered, nor did it speed up his recovery.

Then he ended up with a few blood clots in his leg. Now that was really scary. The clots set him back because his leg swelled so much that he couldn't even walk on it. We did our best to entertain ourselves by pushing him around the house in an office chair. Although I must admit, those 1:00 a.m. pee trips did not thrill me much! However, we got him through these setbacks by continuing to do some light exercise and gentle stretching.

During all this, my back went out on me. Like what happens with most caregivers, I did not get enough rest, exercise, or stretching myself. It got to the point where I couldn't even bend over without holding onto something, and to put my tennis shoes on, I had to sit on the floor and use my arms to pull my legs up so I could tie them. The doctor said I had degenerating discs in my lower back and sent me to physical therapy, which I didn't have time for either. So, I opted to put extra focus on stretching and strengthening my core at home. Again we laughed because we got this mental picture of us in our old age—me pushing Frank around in a wheelchair due to the lasting effect of some injury and me needing the stability of the wheelchair like a walker because my back wouldn't hold me up. We giggled at this future picture as we slowly and painfully went through our stretching and yoga programs at home.

Our recovery goal

We desperately needed something to push for and focus on instead of the current struggle we faced. That is why the first OCR was so important to us. It would be the pinnacle of this struggle to get back into shape and overcome the surgery and the aging process that was now a part of our lives. We needed a goal, but not just any goal; it had to be something we had not accomplished yet, and for us, it had to be a physical challenge. So, in typical Marine fashion, we chose something that would push our bodies physically and challenge us mentally: in stepped the obstacle course races. We ran our first race when Frank was forty-six; I was forty-five.

On an early Saturday morning in September of 2015, we headed to the outskirts of east Little Rock, Arkansas. I am not even sure now where we were, but it was a vast field of waist-high, wheat-colored grass with trees lining parts of the terrain. As we pulled into the parking lot, we saw people climbing over eight-and-a-half-foot walls—five of them lined up in a row like dominos. We watched as participants struggled to jump, pull, climb, scratch, and claw their way over the top of these things, one right after another. I was very excited to be there, but when I turned to Frank after watching this for a while, he laughed and said, *"We'll make it over."* I must have had this look on my face that was a cross between bewilderment and fear that read, *"You've got to be kidding me. We are going over those? What in the world did I sign up for?"*

It was a subdued mood at the starting area, not like the party-it-up mood at the Warrior Dash I had done in May of the previous year. So that made me worry a little bit more. Although the excitement was still there, I must admit that I was nervous and questioned my sanity as I went through the check-in process and found the tent where we deposited our belongings.

Then I saw the first wall. Have you experienced that feeling when you are excited and nervous at the same time? Then you spot the thing you know will be a struggle for you, and it is the first thing you must tackle. You think, *Oh no, I can't possibly do this! What have I gotten myself into?* That was how I felt when I saw the wall we had to conquer to get into the starting pen for this race. You can hear my nervous laugh on the recording I made of others trying to get over that seven-foot wall at the start as I tried to laugh off my anxiety about getting through this race at all.

We watched and discussed our strategy on how we were going to get over this wall as we waited for our turn to go to the starting pen. Then they announce our heat. With nervous excitement, I got in line with the others to start the race and tackle our first obstacle.

Okay, conquering that first wall was quite amusing! I tried running, well, walking really fast, to get the momentum to pull myself over. That didn't work. Then I tried to use the side angles holding up the wall to climb over it. That didn't work either. So, at last, Frank gave my butt a big shove to push me close enough to the top so I could climb and roll over the wall. That would not be the last time, in this or future races, when Frank has had to push my butt over something. I think he secretly, or maybe not so secretly, likes that! But I was now over the wall and in the holding pen. I turned around and watched as Frank swung himself over the top. Dang him! He made it look so easy! I gave him a high five and a friendly scowl then we turned our attention to the announcer, waiting for the gun to go off so we could start the race.

Identify your goal

When recovering from an injury or a setback of any kind, it's helpful to select a recovery goal and to identify what steps you must take to get there. Having that carrot, something you strive for, makes putting in the work to get there more bearable. It also helps to define how you will go through the Recovery process. To complete an OCR, we not only had to get back into physical shape, but Frank also had to recover from his surgery, and I had to focus on strengthening my back. Sticking with our exercise routine was easier when we had a goal and knew what we had to work on to complete an obstacle course race. It helped us narrow our focus, plan the steps we must take, and remove distractions. We knew we had to exercise and get stronger to succeed in a physically demanding challenge.

The goal you identify must resonate with you and align with your Recovery objective. It must be realistic, and the time you allot must be sufficient, given the goal you are striving for and the injury you are recovering from. Otherwise, you will get discouraged. Once you have set a goal, make the plan to reach that goal easy to follow, and try not to have any unrealistic steps that will cause you to give up on your recovery goal. They must be simple to follow but challenging enough to create progress in your healing. You also want to incorporate them into your daily habits to help you stick with them. If the steps are too challenging or difficult to fit into your schedule, you might give up, which would mean not meeting your end goal, thus sabotaging your recovery.

It's challenging to provide goal examples because the physical or mental injury you have is personal, and many things could be the goals that will start you on your Recovery journey. But it is worth the effort to explore what might be the ideal carrot on the stick for you to begin the process and motivate you to move forward. Since I based this entire book on obstacle courses, I will use a physical challenge for my example here.

Let's say you are recovering from an injury and have a realistic goal of running a 5 km race. If you have ever trained for a 5 km, 10 km, half-marathon, or marathon, you know you need to log the miles to survive the race. If you haven't, then trust me on this. You need to log the miles. Depending on the distance of the race and how far in the future the race is, you will need to structure your training so that you can meet the number of miles of your chosen race. If you are recovering from an injury, you will also want to take into account the time you need to heal.

One way to calculate the time you need is to work backward from the race date, using an app or someone's spreadsheet (my personal favorite) to know how many miles you need to log each week and what days you need to do so. This also helps you to understand how long it will take to train and heal so that you can be at your best on race day.

Each day, you use the app or look on your spreadsheet to know what you are doing that day and the next. Because of your plan, you will know how many miles you need to log and whether this is a run, walk, interval, or rest day; in other words, keep it easy. You already planned what to do, so you have no decision to make, and you only need to follow the steps, one day at a time. If you include this in your routine (e.g., every morning before breakfast), it will be easier to stick to the schedule—even when the miles increase. Training may still suck at times, but you know what you must do; it is part of your routine. If you do not do it, you know it will make the next day more challenging, and you may even feel a little guilty because you didn't check the box off that day. The great thing about following a plan is that if you stick with it, you have a better chance of reaching your goal.

You can handle obstacles in life in the same manner. If you know you have something to overcome, what goal can you identify to help you meet the challenge? Think through your obstacle. What objective makes sense? What will correlate well with the steps to overcome what you face? For instance, we had to not only heal, but we also had to get into shape to participate in the OCR. We had to work on our strength, flexibility, and endurance. It would not have made sense to only walk and stretch. Although that might have helped our endurance some, we couldn't do half the obstacles on the course without some sort of strength training.

Maybe it is a work project or a sales goal. What steps need to be taken each day to move you closer to the end goal or completing the project? For sales, it might be the number of calls or meetings you need to do each day. For a project, it could be the tasks that need to be done to meet the specific stage of the project. Working backward from the end date or sales goal helps you to identify what steps need to be taken and how long they might take. Following the steps you have identified makes the process feel less overwhelming and gives you objectives to meet to move you forward toward your goal.

This can also be applied to a financial goal, such as eliminating debt, saving for retirement, or buying a new house. If your goal is to be debt-free, you need to know what you owe so you can plan a strategy to pay everything off. The strategy could be to make a payment schedule and identify when you can increase your payment amount. This will help you move toward your goal of eliminating debt and give you a plan to follow because you can track your progress.

Identify milestones

You should also plan little wins throughout the process—milestones that will make you feel like you are making progress toward your goal. One of my favorite half-marathon prep programs in northwest Arkansas had specific public distance races that correlated with the training schedule. These gave us little wins and accomplishments that made the training more fun and less daunting as the miles got longer. Plus, we got some *bling* to add to our wall! More about the bling later. Your milestones will vary based on your recovery goal. Physical milestones might be pounds lost, better-fitting clothes, the ability to lift heavier weights, the number of days you chose healthy food, or days you went to bed earlier to get more sleep.

If you are working on a financial goal such as eliminating debt, each time you pay off a credit card, have a cut-up-the-card party and celebrate by cutting up the credit card and throwing it away. Thus, you mark another milestone in your overall goal of getting out of debt.

You can also enlist the help of friends and family on your journey toward achieving your goal. Accountability groups with weekly or bi-weekly check-ins work well for this. Your accountability partners must understand you are working toward something important to you. Make sure they are willing and open to being on the journey with you to provide you with support and encouragement along the way. The point is to make mini celebrations out of these milestones. They are to encourage, not discourage, you as you work on reaching your bigger goal.

The First Wall

Don't let it surprise you if you hit that first wall and start questioning your sanity. We all do! Any challenge or obstacle you take on will always be difficult at first. You will have obstacles to overcome throughout the process, and the first one is the hardest because you are just getting started. A little shove in the butt might help you get over it and give you forward momentum. Don't forget what you are striving for, the goal you want to accomplish, or why you want to recover. Most importantly, don't let this first wall stop you from going after your goals. You know it is going to be there, so be ready to take it on!

You will be nervous, scared, worried, and maybe even a little excited as you start down the path toward your goal. Use that energy to help move you forward over that first wall. Embrace it and run with it. It is part of the energy of the journey you are about to go on!

Lesson

- Identifying what you want to recover from
- Set a goal that will motivate you
- Establish a plan to recover

Take Action

What do you need to recover from? Is it minor, or is it big? Is it a physical or a mental challenge or both? We all have something that is holding us back in some way. Is there something that you could strive for to set you on the path to Recovery? Is there a focus, a goal you would like to accomplish? Is there an obstacle you want to, or maybe need to, take on or overcome?

Take a moment to describe what you need to Recover from and what goal will help you move forward. Using the questions below, describe what it is, how it will help you recover, and why it is important to you.

Questions to Ponder

- What goal or accomplishment would motivate you to look at this challenge differently?
- What would help you focus your recovery efforts?
- What would accomplishing this challenge or goal look like to you?
- How would you feel if you achieved it?
- What do you need to do to accomplish this challenge or goal?

Identify the steps it would take to get you there, then break them down into manageable pieces. Don't worry so much about getting them perfect. All you need to do is have a rough outline of the overall process, then clearly identify the first couple of steps you need to take to start you down the path. The next ones will come into focus once you get started.

After you have your goal in mind, you need to climb that first wall—you need to get into that holding pen so you can start the race! But be prepared for setbacks. It would be nice if your goals could be accomplished without stumbling blocks, but that is not how life works. Next, we will go into strategies to help you overcome life's unexpected obstacles.

2

TARZAN SWING

How do you face disappointment?

Why do we fall? So, we can learn to pick ourselves back up.

—Batman, *The Dark Knight*

As we stood in the holding pen at the starting line, waiting for the countdown to send us on our way, I didn't know Frank had hurt himself on that first wall. He wouldn't admit this to me until we had started the race and were running through a field toward our first obstacle. That is when he turned to me and said, *"I think I pulled something in my left shoulder on the first wall."* We wouldn't figure out how severe the damage was until a year and another obstacle course race later, but his injury would interfere with the rest of our race that day.

The first few obstacles we encountered were not too bad. They involved some balancing and climbing, but overall, we got through them, even with Frank's hurt arm. Then we came to the Tarzan Swing. You might remember these swings from your long-ago playground days. I am not sure they still have them on playgrounds these days, but when we were growing up, we raced to swing on them at recess after lunch. This obstacle is set up with rings that vary in size and shape at the end of chains attached in a row to a pole above. You swing from one to the next, hand over hand, to get to the other side. Easy enough, right? Well, maybe not so easy. The Tarzan Swing in this Conquer the Gauntlet race is this simple of a design set over a pit of muddy water. To add to the fun, they set the rings at different heights with varying lengths between them. The goal is to swing from one to the next, hoping you have enough momentum, strength, and arm's length to grab the next ring. If you drop, you end up in the muddy water pit below and must swim to the other side. They set up many obstacles like this, and if you do not complete the challenge, you end up in the mirky water below.

Frank went first, feeling confident he could master this swinging obstacle despite his hurt left arm. He grabbed the first ring with his right arm, then reached for the second ring without a problem. Halfway through his swing to the third ring, he dropped into the water. I was next in line to tackle this obstacle, so watching him fall after only two rings didn't give me much confidence that I could complete this challenge. If Frank couldn't get across with his upper body strength, I was sure that I wouldn't. Plus, I realized then that I wasn't mentally or physically prepared for this obstacle. It had been a very long time since I had swung from monkey bars, never mind rings, and we didn't include them in our training.

I reached for the first ring from the platform, extending my left hand as far as I could while on my toes and holding onto the wooden pole that supported the structure with my right hand. Then I took a slight hop off the platform and grabbed it with both hands. I had no real momentum, so I ended up slightly swinging from the ring, holding on with both hands. I couldn't get enough momentum, strength, or confidence to reach for the next one. After a few moments of hanging from that ring, I had to decide whether to return to the platform and start again or drop into the water. However, I couldn't reach the platform, and the line of people waiting on me was growing, so I opted to drop into the water.

As I swam to the other side where Frank was waiting for me, I kicked myself for not being strong enough or mentally prepared to tackle such an elementary-school obstacle. It was not a simple obstacle, but I couldn't help thinking that I used to swing from those things all the time as a kid. Why was I having such a hard time now? My inability to muster the strength to conquer them again as an adult disappointed me.

As Frank helped me get out of the water, my focus turned from myself to him as I noticed something was off. He winced when he helped me out of the water, and he held his left arm in a sling position. Frank told me he felt something tear and heard a pop when he swung on his left arm. That is why he had to drop into the water. His left arm couldn't hold him when all his weight was on it. That slight pull he had felt when he hoisted himself over the first wall turned into a significant issue on the Tarzan Swing. And it would prevent him from doing most of the remaining obstacles on the course that day.

Handling disappointment

This realization was disappointing to Frank, more than my disappointment about not swinging from the rings as I did as a kid. His disappointment wasn't because he wasn't strong enough or prepared to take on the challenge. It was that something happened that he couldn't control or prevent. Further, it was something he couldn't overcome that day. He had to accept it and do what he could to make the best of the rest of the obstacle course because we were only about a quarter of the way through it. We still had a long way to go to finish the race. I asked if he wanted to stop and turn back or get help. But true to his Marine training, that was not an option; we had to finish the course. Frank would do his best to get through the obstacles he could and would walk around the others, but he would finish what he started. He would finish the race.

As we moved through the rest of the obstacles that day, Frank's arm got worse, and he couldn't do the obstacles that would have been easy for him without his injury. It was a massive letdown for both of us, given all we had been through that year and a half of his recovery from brain surgery. But to his credit, he stayed and continued the race, doing all the obstacles he could, and continued to shove my butt over the ones I struggled with. He still had one good arm, after all!

Frank is always quoting movie lines. One of his favorites is from *Galaxy Quest,* when the character Jason Nesmith, as Commander Peter Quincy Taggart, proclaims, *"Never give up. Never surrender!"*[2] whenever his sci-fi crew faces adversity. Frank says it often enough when any of us are facing a challenge that our children can finish the quote and know Dad will accept nothing but a completed task, even when only cleaning their rooms. You must complete the mission!

The quote is about more than completing the mission, though. If you look at it another way, you see it is more about overcoming whatever challenge you face and doing so with the determination that you can get the job done. Adversity will not stop you. It might slow you down or cause you to do things differently than you had thought you would, but it will not prevent you from completing your mission. You might not like it, and it might disappoint you if things don't go the way you wanted them to, but you will follow through and complete the mission. The quote addresses *how* you face your challenges and disappointments.

When Frank admitted he had hurt himself, he struggled with his disappointment that the race was not going as he had envisioned. He had planned, trained, and worked hard to prepare for this OCR. This race was what he had focused on throughout his Recovery process. It motivated him to do the hard recovery work. So at first, Frank was in denial that his arm was even hurt or that it was severe enough to prevent him from completing the challenges on the course. When the reality of his situation hit him, he had a choice to make. Frank could give up and quit the race, or he could tackle the manageable obstacles and make the most of the rest of the course and the day. He chose the latter—not giving up. Frank had to adjust his plan for the day, but he continued forward. Best of all, for both of us, he continued forward with a positive attitude, made the most of the challenges he could do, and helped me when I needed it.

FACING YOUR REALITY

I did not sustain any injuries, but I faced other self-realizations that day. I realized that I had to work harder to have the physical or mental strength I once had. Also, I found I was more concerned about hurting myself than I thought I would be. But the realization that shocked me the most was my lack of confidence in my ability to do things I should be able to do or could have done at one time. I was no longer as fearless as I used to be. I even feared obstacles I should have been able to handle. Although I know I would never do a Gladiator-type race as you see on TV, many challenges on these courses are doable for most weekend warriors. They would have been manageable for me just five years back, but now I questioned if I could do them at all. And I was also concerned I would get hurt doing them. This realization nagged at me through the rest of the course and afterward. But it also challenged me; I knew I must face it and do something about it.

Even though we both faced some disappointments that day, Frank and I didn't let it stop us from attempting every obstacle we could. Most importantly, we had fun. We laughed and poked fun at each other and ourselves when we got stuck, and we finished the course with smiles on our faces.

Salvage what you can

We'll dig deeper into what happens when things don't go your way in Chapter 12—Virtual Races. But for now, the lesson from this part of our journey involves your immediate response to things that do not go as you thought they would. A viable option for us was to quit at any point on the course, and we had a good reason to do so with Frank's injured arm, but we didn't. We stuck with it that day and made the most of it.

So my question for you is: what happens when something derails a part of your day, event, or task you are doing? What is your immediate reaction? What emotions are you tackling? Do you try to salvage what you can, make some adjustments, and find a different way, or do you get upset, mad, or sad?

Often in our lives, something minor (or maybe not so insignificant at the time) changes how we handle a task or obstacle. You might be behind a slow car on the freeway when you are already late. A potential client asks to postpone a meeting, or the school calls because your child is sick and needs a ride home. These sudden, unexpected occurrences can change your plans for the day or maybe interfere with you meeting your project deadline. Many little things can disrupt a day and derail you—if you let them.

How you face these challenges can set the tone for the rest of your day, week, or even year. And if you let them get out of control, they can have a lasting negative effect, not just on that day but on your life and those around you. You retain your power over your day by how you react to things that are out of your control. By taking responsibility for your reactions, you regain control. When you regain control of the situation, you give yourself hope, which helps put things in a better light so you can see the path forward.

Pay attention to how you react when things do not go the way you planned. What is your gut reaction? How do you handle the change in plans? Or the disruption? Things will not always go the way you had envisioned. Life likes to throw you curveballs. Learn to adjust and make the most of the situation despite the disruptions. And remember: these events, or disruptions, may define the moment, but they do not define who you are—unless you allow them to.

Lesson

- Identify how you react when things don't go as planned
- Gain control of your emotions
- Salvage what you can

Take Action

Think about a time when something unexpected derailed your plans for the day or maybe the week. What was your immediate reaction? When you look back at past events or obstacles that threw a wrench into your plans, what did you do to adjust and get through the day the best that you could? How did you react? What could you have done better or wish you would have done better? How can you prepare yourself for the next time? Because you know there will be a next time.

What you focus on becomes your reality. How can you adjust your focus to lead you to a positive outcome or experience?

Questions to Ponder:

- How do you handle unexpected events?
- How would you like to handle them?
- Is there a disconnect?
- What could you do to adjust to changing events in a more positive way?
- What can you focus on?
- What will help you to adjust to life's fluctuations in a way that does not derail the rest of your day?
- What emotions are you feeling?
- Do you have a way to get through the emotions so you can see the other side? Like taking a walk, breathing exercises, a good cry, or something else to release the emotional steam valve.

Knowing what your immediate reactions are and how to manage them is the start to overcoming the obstacles in your path. In the last part of Recovery, we will discuss why it is important to understand what is holding you back, how taking a step back to re-evaluate the situation will help you move forward, and what to do when those voices of negativity pop into your head.

3
GAUNTLET 2.0

How do you overcome?

Harder. You are stronger than this, Diana.

—Antiope, *Wonder Woman*

On the day of that first obstacle course race in 2015, both Frank and I faced some enormous disappointments. We were both frustrated, but for different reasons. I wasn't as strong or as confident in my abilities as I used to be, and Frank's injury prevented him from doing what he wanted to do. Most of all, though, it humbled us. We were turning a corner in our lives and had an important decision to make. Should we forego some activities we would have been able to do a few years ago? Or do we work harder so we can continue to do them? Looking back now, it was a significant turning point in our lives.

Frank and I licked our mental and physical wounds, and we set out to do better next time. We decided we would not give up or give in; we were here to fight, get stronger, and try again. But we had to take a different approach than before to tackle a few things in this next Recovery phase so we could take on our next race. Unlike recovering from a major setback, such as brain surgery, this one was minor in comparison, yet it felt enormous in the challenge it presented.

First, Frank had to focus on getting his left arm back into shape, which meant some downtime, once again, to allow his arm to heal. He didn't like that very much; however, he knew it was the right thing to do. My focus was on increasing both my physical and mental strength. I should have been able to take on many challenges we had faced in our first obstacle course race, regardless of my physical strength. For it wasn't my physical strength that held me back, but my lack of confidence in my ability and my fear of getting hurt.

We will dig into a few key things going on here. They include how you recover from setbacks (multiple times), face the aging process, and gain confidence in your ability despite the reasons you, or others, think you shouldn't or can't do something.

Recovering—Again!

Are there times when you feel you just can't get a break? That each time you overcome an obstacle, another one is there waiting for you? That is how Frank felt. He found the time he needed to recover maddening. He had just spent a year recovering from brain surgery only to be down for the count again. However, his arm was of no use to him, so that forced him to take it easy if he wanted full use of his arm again.

Frank also wasn't a big fan of the less intense workouts, even though he knew they would help him recover. It took some coercing, but he slowed down enough to work on his flexibility, especially in his shoulders. It was a significant change from the way he usually attempted to recover from his injuries, which was no recovery at all—pushing harder was his motto. Now, however, the ticking clock of age proved that this philosophy no longer served him well—as if it did when we were younger!

So once again, as we did after his brain surgery, we slowly worked to regain strength and flexibility in our bodies. After a few months, Frank could use his arm again, allowing us to add strength training to our workout routine. Frank's arm still bothered him at times. We wouldn't know the full extent of the damage until a year later, when we found out he had torn his bicep, leading him to another surgery. At this point, though, I am not sure what bothered him more: his injured arm, the downtime to recover again, the slower healing process, or all of the above.

Pushing through

Any time over these many years, Frank could have given up on recovering from an injury. His fortitude to push on and recover amazes me. He gets a little grumpy and mopey sometimes because it frustrates him. Who wouldn't feel like that with the constant rebuilding and recovery process? But he keeps at it. Frank has had every reason not to go to the gym, lift another weight, go for a run, or do anything physical. But he keeps at it. Maybe my husband is stubborn, or it could be the Marine in him. Quite possibly, it is both, but I think the real reason is that he doesn't want to give up or give in. Remember the quote from Cmdr. Taggart, "Never give up. Never surrender." That is his motto.

Once, when I asked how he works through things when he has an injury, Frank told me he thinks of a three-legged dog. The dog doesn't know he only has three legs and is not looking at other dogs, wishing he could have his fourth leg. On his own, he learns how to walk, run, sit, and stand with his three legs and still wags his tail when he sees his people. That the dog has but three legs doesn't make him stop enjoying life and doing what he can to keep up with his people. He does it without thinking. So that is what Frank does—he keeps at it. And, as discussed in the previous chapter, he maintains a good attitude.

However, even this positive attitude didn't keep him from getting frustrated and impatient about having to step back to heal again. The part of this mental challenge we will focus on here is taking the time to heal and why it is imperative to do so.

The Importance of Rest

As we age, it is easy to feel disappointed that it takes longer to recover from hard workouts or injuries than it used to. We may even wonder if we are getting too old to take on certain challenges. Pondering if we should succumb to these setbacks and stop working to regain the spirit, strength, or flexibility of our youth. It is tempting to listen to others or the voices in our heads, who tell us constantly that *you just can't do the things you used to,* or *that's for younger folks.* When we start believing them, we allow these voices to be our excuses for not trying harder or even trying at all.

We must develop the mental fortitude to overcome this aging challenge and the voices. To do so, you must first understand why rest is necessary, no matter how old or young you are. It is the only way your body will heal itself. Second, don't let the ticking clock be your excuse to not even attempt to recover, get back out there again, or try new things.

Take a Pause

Our bodies are amazing machines. If given enough time, rest, and nourishment, we can come back from almost anything. Rest makes all the difference in whether we will heal the way we need to in harmony with our physical design. Not only is it okay to let our bodies rest, but it is necessary for recovery. If done right, we will not lose ground in our training, gain back the weight we worked so hard to lose, or lose the muscle tone we worked so hard to gain. Studies show we can actually gain ground by resting.

In their book *Peak Performance: Elevate Your Game, Avoid Burnout, and Thrive with the New Science of Success*, Brad Stulbery and Steve Magness discuss how extended rest periods and breaks in training schedules allow top athletes to avoid burnout, stay healthy, and increase their performance.[3] One of the athletes they interviewed has used this rest technique for years, allowing him to remain a top competitor into his forties. And I bet into his fifties as well! The other benefits to rest days or periods are the promotion of muscle recovery and preventing the damaging effects of overtraining.

Like many people, my husband has difficulty with this. Resting or pressing the pause button in the workout schedule for more than a day has him thinking he will lose all the ground he has gained. Convincing him otherwise is a constant battle. The same can be said about any setback in life, not only physical ones. Sometimes pausing to evaluate a situation or retool a project is what is needed to move forward. No one likes it much. It can cost time and money. But the outcome can be so much better. And you just might find you are further along than you thought you would be, and it didn't cost as much as you thought it might.

It seems we have lost our patience with the process of healing and have forgotten that change doesn't happen overnight. We find it difficult to take a step back from the constant push forward and to focus more on the process of healing. Healing our bodies, our minds, our jobs, our families, and our relationships. Taking a pause doesn't mean giving up. It means allowing time to let nature take its course. To think through the situation and evaluate your options. But it doesn't mean sitting on the couch eating bonbons either!

SMALL STEPS FORWARD

I like to call it active healing. When you are recovering from a physical injury, do the work to keep your body moving forward. You may not be able to run, but can you walk? Or bike? Is physical therapy needed or stretching or yoga? Understand what your limitations are and work with them, not against them. Do what you can while allowing your body to heal. Many studies have proven that doing so will get you back to where you were much faster and possibly in better shape than before.

Maybe you have had a setback with your career, passed over for a promotion, or lost your job. Instead of ignoring the setback by binge-watching your favorite program, what skills can you learn? What courses or classes can you take to improve your resume? What books will help you reset your mind or your attitude, or both? Are there mentors or coaches you can connect with to help you focus your efforts? Each time you have a setback, it is an opportunity to evaluate where you are at, where you want to go, and what it will take to get you there.

With our relationships, sometimes the pause allows time for you to process, forgive, forget, or calm down. I have learned with our kids that by taking a pause when they do something they are not supposed to do, I am a much better parent when resolving the situation. I let my frustration subside (heal), then I can act with more patience and less yelling. Same with my husband. Love the guy dearly, but sometimes he frustrates the heck out of me. It is at these times that taking a step back to allow my feelings to relax gives me a cooler head, allowing me to have a more rational conversation. It helps him too!

There are many times in life when a pause button is needed. Where we need to reset ourselves and our lives. This is a necessary part of life. Just as we pass through the seasons each year, our lives have seasons too. The wintertime is a period of rest and rejuvenation, but remember that every year, spring is right around the corner. It doesn't matter how old you get; each spring is a time to start again and take on your next challenge.

Speaking of age, let's tackle that next!

BATTLING AGISM

In our mid-forties, we also faced the aging dilemma. We didn't want to accept the idea that we couldn't do things as well as we used to. A rest and recovery break felt like an admission that we were getting older. We didn't like that at all! Not one bit. We needed to change our thought processes here as well. It's not that we *couldn't* do the things we once were able to do, but that we needed to change our strategy so that we *could*. Through this journey, we accepted that fact and are now stronger and fitter in our fifties than we were before. Plus, we can still do the things we did when we were younger, and we are even doing some things that we didn't do. So much for those who say you can't teach old dogs new tricks! Ha!

Age is just a number. I am not sure where we got the idea that as we get older, we shouldn't or couldn't do the things we did when we were younger. That our time has passed, we should be happy to sit in our rocking chairs and let our bodies and minds fade away. Times are changing, though, and many of us "older" folks are realizing that the ticking clock doesn't need to be a ticking time bomb blowing away our opportunities of doing the things we want to do. Despite what others might think.

I got so frustrated at an emoji I saw one day when I went through a workout app. To select my age range (50–55), my choice was a grandma-looking emoji. I couldn't even bring myself to click on it! I closed the app and decided I didn't need that workout app anyway. I lift more weight now in my fifties than I did in my twenties; I was not interested in an app that would put me in a box with others my age and tell me what I could and could not do. No way!

But that's the problem. How many of us would have gone ahead and clicked on that age emoji, thinking that is all they are supposed to do at their age? Now, it might be right for some, but should it be right for all? And does it need to be? The same can be said for starting a business or starting over in a new career. Starting over in a new relationship. Why do we put ourselves in a box and limit what we can do because we are at a certain age? Why do others think less of us as we get older? Either at the office or in the gym.

We are constantly surprising people when we tell them our age on the course. In one race, we struck up a conversation with a group of ladies after one of them said, *"I am getting too old for this."* I asked her how old she was, and she admitted that she had just turned forty. I smiled and told her that we were over fifty. They were shocked! Why? Why can't you continue to do things as you get older? Why is that so shocking? It shouldn't be.

There is no reason for us to think that our advancing age should be the death knell to our opportunities in life. I challenge you to rethink your aging process and stop letting the voices in your head or from others tell you what you can or cannot do. We didn't when we were younger—why would we do this to ourselves as we get older? As much as this bothers me now, it took me a while to come to this realization. This was the mental gymnastics I was going through at this point in our journey.

The other mental games we play

Frank's mental challenge was acknowledging it was not only okay but also necessary to let his body rest and recover. My mental challenge was gaining the confidence in my ability to tackle some of the obstacles on the course. It could be his Marine training, but Frank never seemed to doubt that he could conquer certain obstacles or take on any challenge the course threw at him. As for me, I was taking on some activities I had never done before, pushing my body and mind to tackle new challenges. Also, I did this beyond the age when people think they should slow down and not climb trees anymore. A topic we just discussed.

I wanted to take on these challenges to test my fortitude and know that I pushed myself to keep trying and growing. To do this, I focused on increasing my physical and mental strength, which meant I had to face down the demons of self-doubt. *Can I make that jump? Can I climb that wall? What happens if I hurt myself? What if I can't pull myself over an obstacle?*

I still work on some of those doubts. But with each course we take on, I get better and gain more confidence. That is the key here. You gain confidence each time you do something. If you never try something or attempt to tackle a challenge, you will never know the mental fortitude you have or how well you will do. Self-doubt and worry hold you back from tackling many things in life.

Each time I do an obstacle course challenge, I complete more of the obstacles. I think that progress is part of what brings me back each time. While the physical challenges in the race also draw me back, the challenge within me to test my resolve and face my fear does so even more. The training I do between races is not only to keep me physically fit, but I also work on the areas I have identified as weak or necessary to complete more obstacles, such as pull-ups. I still struggle with pull-ups, but I do them. There are some obstacles that I will never do, and I will explain that in Chapter 5, "Pegatron." But I work to continue to build confidence in my ability to do the ones I have identified as doable.

We all have personal challenges to overcome as we face obstacles in life. Life is not perfect, but we can take what we have and build on it. It's important to identify your weaknesses, then work on them. You also need to know your strengths and capitalize on them. That is what I did during this recovery period, so I could take on another OCR and conquer more obstacles. I focused on areas where I was the weakest and used my strengths to work on them. When I made this change to my training, I gained the confidence I needed to not only take on the challenges of the course that I knew I could do but to take on more challenges in life.

Adjustments Fuels Confidence

A change for me was to add more weight training. My prior workout regimen was comprised of a lot of running and cardio routines, with some strength training mixed in. Lifting was somewhat intimidating to me. However, I realized if I wanted to do certain obstacles, I must work on my strength, so I hit the weights. I had to overcome my avoidance and anxiety about it.

With this change in my training, I had a rather interesting realization. As I had hoped, my increased physical strength gave me more confidence to overcome some more obstacles on the course. But it also gave me the confidence to take on other challenges in my life, like leaving a cushy, well-paying job to start my business. It was the process of strength training that gave me this confidence. It was not the muscles that did it, although that was a nice by-product, but confidence in myself. As I built my self-confidence through my workouts by pushing myself to lift heavier weights, facing something that had once intimidated me, that belief in myself poured over into other things in my life.

Forcing yourself to do what stretches you builds your self-confidence. If you face and prevail over a tough challenge, your confidence in facing another hard challenge increases. That is nothing new, maybe only a different way to look at it. As I worked through my training and did the exercises I hadn't done before, such as lifting heavier weights, my confidence grew enough to try another obstacle on the course. I also grew in my ability to take on more challenges in my life. My willingness to do something new and challenging expanded my belief in what I could do. That happens when you take on a new challenge in work or life. Each time you do something that stretches you or makes you face doubt and conquer it, you increase your mental strength. The training you do between challenges prepares you to perform better, which gives you the confidence to take on the next one. It has a snowball effect. One you might not even realize you are doing or have done before.

With each heavier weight I lifted and each OCR we did, I found I was challenging my thinking about age and other things in life. I stopped questioning if I was getting too weak to take on physical challenges. If I was too old to begin a new business venture. Had that ship already sailed? Well, I realized I am not dead—not yet, not even close. I have two teenagers at home and a lot of life ahead of me. Why shouldn't I accept these challenges? Why shouldn't you? Should we let people, the world, and society tell us what we should or cannot do or how we should or shouldn't act at certain ages? Even though I could be a grandmother at my age, I don't feel old, and I won't let someone tell me I am too old to do something—not even me! Sometimes you must play hardball with yourself and question what is holding you back. Is it realistic, or is it in your mind?

Unlike the three-legged dog, we are usually the ones holding ourselves back. We should all remember the three-legged dog when we feel we can't do something that we actually can. Instead of focusing on why we *can't*, we need to focus on why we *can*.

Don't let your fears hold you back. Instead . . . be the dog!

Lesson

- Rest, Restore, & Rebuild
- Identify what is holding you back
- Battle that voice in your head, in your family, in society

Take Action

Think back to a time when an injury or something in life set you back. What emotions did you feel? How did you react? Most importantly, how did you move forward? Or did you? Why or why not?

Now, describe a time when you let something hold you back from taking on a challenge. What was it, and what impact did it have on you?

Using the questions below, describe what it is, what you feel is holding you back, and what you think it will take to help you overcome this obstacle/challenge in your life.

Questions to Ponder

- What do you do to allow yourself time to heal?
- If you do not, how could you benefit from some brief downtime?
- If you do, how do you rebuild your body and mind?
- How do you build confidence in yourself so you can take on life's challenges?
- What is holding you back?
- What stories are you telling yourself that enforce the feeling that you cannot do something?
- What can you replace these stories with?

These past chapters focused on what it takes to recover and get back into the game of life. In the next section, we will discuss discovering what your reason is for taking on a challenge, why you should or shouldn't take something on, and how you take on those yucky tasks in life.

PART 2
Discovery

4

THE CONTINENTAL DIVIDE

WHAT IS YOUR PURPOSE?

It's about what you believe. And I believe in love. Only love will truly save the world.

—Wonder Woman, *Wonder Woman*

For the rest of the book, we will focus on specific obstacles that we have encountered over the years and discuss the lessons we took away from each one. Many of these obstacles we faced multiple times, which is part of the training these lessons provide: not every obstacle is conquered on your first attempt. Sometimes you need to find a compelling reason for doing something, so you can find the fortitude to overcome that obstacle. This became crystal clear to me on the Continental Divide.

In the Conquer the Gauntlet OCR, they have an obstacle set up like an A-Frame structure with a wall on one side and slats on the other. The goal is to use a rope to climb up the face of the wall, heave yourself over the top, then climb down the slats on the other side. The Warrior Dash OCR had a similar obstacle with some slight modifications that made it easier to tackle. First, the ropes have knots in them, and there are slats across the face of the wall so you can use them to help you climb up the wall and over the top. In the Gauntlet, there are no slats on the wall or knots in the rope, so it is up to you to get yourself up the wall, using the rope to climb to the top and hoist yourself over it, then climb down the slats on the other side.

In our first Conquer the Gauntlet OCR in Little Rock, Arkansas, in 2015, the year after Frank recovered from brain surgery, we hit that obstacle after he had already damaged his left arm. So he couldn't even climb up the wall with the rope, much less pull himself over the top. Since my husband couldn't attempt this obstacle, I pretty much gave up on it. I tried to climb the wall once but didn't get very far. I ended up hanging from the rope, lying flat against the wall. I had to slide down the face of the wall holding onto the rope to keep myself from smacking to the ground. In short, I had no compelling reason to climb the wall and heave myself over it. In my mind, there was nothing at the top for me, nothing on the other side, and no motivation for me to put myself through the pain or effort to do it. With a wave of my hand and a drop in my shoulders, I walked around it with my husband.

But that wall haunted me! I didn't like that I had walked around the wall, not even trying to get over it. Instead, I gave up on myself way too soon, and because my husband couldn't get over it, I used that as my excuse not to even try. Sound familiar? The thing is, I knew I could make it over if I had only tried harder. That is what truly haunted me.

A SECOND CHANCE

We were in Tulsa, Oklahoma, in 2016 when we met the Continental Divide again. My husband had worked on healing his shoulder, so it was in good shape for this OCR, and we were ready to go! We had been through the course before and were now more familiar with this race and its obstacles. However, because the location had changed, the terrain and the layout of the obstacles were a little different from Little Rock, Arkansas. By this second encounter with the Continental Divide, we had completed about half of the four-mile course and had to climb up an enormous hill to get to the Divide. The curators of this fine event thought it a great idea to put this obstacle at the highest point in Tulsa! Yeah, great idea!

This time, though, I was determined to get over the wall! And now that I had my strong man with me, I had no excuse not to! Up and over went Frank. It was way too easy for him, mind you, which did annoy me a little. Now it was my turn. With Frank waiting at the top for me, I told myself, *I got this,* as I started climbing the rope. But as I got close to the top, I ran out of strength to pull myself up any further.

To appreciate the difficulty level of this challenge, you should know that they secure the rope just over the top of the A-frame. So, by the time you get to the top, it is pretty much flat against the wall, with little play between the wall and the rope. Thus, it makes it difficult to use anything but your upper body strength to pull you up and over. You can imagine that without significant upper-body strength, getting yourself over the top is challenging. Upper-body strength is my weakness for several reasons, as it is for most women. Our center of gravity is in our hips, and most of our strength is in our legs, not our upper body and arms. Before that event, I had not yet added upper-body strength training to my workout regimen.

Knowing this, you might see why I was now hanging at the top of the rope against the wall and could not reach over the top of the A-Frame to get a grasp to pull myself up. I also didn't have the strength and couldn't get enough leverage to get my feet or knees under me so I could lean out some and try to crawl up the wall any further. My two options were to find the strength to pull myself up further or slide back down the wall. I couldn't pull myself up or reach Frank's outstretched hand, so my only option was to slide down and try again.

So, I eased myself down the front of the wall, dusted myself off at the bottom, and told myself again that *I can do this*. This time, I had more momentum and determination to get far enough up the wall for my husband to help me over. Although this attempt was more successful, and I made it to the top of the wall, I was stuck again. My head and shoulders were above the top of the A-frame, and I was in a chicken-wing position, holding onto the top with my arms as the rest of my body hung down the front of the wall. Because of my position, I couldn't figure out how to pull myself over all the way, but this time my husband was there.

"What can I do?" he asked.

"Pull me over."

"But I do not want to hurt you." Frank would have to grab my arms and drag me over the top, and he was kind to consider that. My reply, however, was quite strong.

"I DON'T CARE! PULL ME THE @#$% OVER!!" I think I was frustrated by then, and I didn't want to slide back down again. So, with my husband's help and bruised arms and chest, I got over the Divide on my second attempt.

Accepting Help

My husband still feels bad that he bruised my arms by pulling me over, but that didn't bother me so much as getting stuck again. I was thankful he was there, but I still hadn't conquered that obstacle by myself. I know there are some obstacles in these races and in life that we need help with, and I accept that. The help is necessary sometimes, and we will cover that in detail in later chapters. So I really shouldn't have been frustrated about needing the help. I had not done enough upper-body strength training to pull myself over the wall, and I lacked confidence in my ability to do so.

The same is true for the obstacles we encounter in life. Needing help is not a bad thing, even if you feel you should be able to handle the situation on your own. Sometimes, having a little guidance can make all the difference between success and failure. It can teach you how it feels to accomplish the task at hand, show you a new way to tackle the problem, or how to power through the obstacle. It might not be pretty, but you get through it, and you learn what it feels like to accomplish the task. Which gives you confidence to take it on again or take on another obstacle.

As for this one, though, I still hadn't found it in me to tackle that beast on my own. I still didn't have a reason strong enough to allow my fortitude to shine through and conquer that thing. That's why this obstacle still haunted me.

IT'S NOT ABOUT YOU

But that would not be the last time our paths would cross! The next time, I had my 12-year-old daughter with me. So, the challenge was no longer about *me* getting over the Divide; it was about *my daughter* getting over it. That is where the strength of your purpose or your why comes in. If you find your purpose for doing something, it can provide you with a ton of motivation you might not otherwise have. We mention the topic often because it is such a powerful concept. When you see it in action in your life, it can give you the power to lift cars off people like Superman! Well, maybe not. Sometimes, though, our purpose shows up as a quiet feeling rather than a slap-you-across-the-face moment like in the V8™ commercials.

For our third encounter with the Continental Divide, I found my purpose for tackling this obstacle. However, the profoundness of it only dawned on me after the fact. By then in our OCR journey, my husband had shoulder and bicep surgery (yes, we can rebuild him), and both our kids had now joined us on this crazy adventure of ours. It was 2018, two years after our last Conquer the Gauntlet challenge, and we were back in Tulsa, Oklahoma, standing in front of the Continental Divide yet again.

Our fourteen-year-old son and my husband were attempting the right side of the Divide, while my daughter and I stuck to the left side. Oh, I didn't share that there is even more diabolical fun to the obstacle than earlier explained! Well, let me share. On the right side of the wall, there are ropes as well, but they dangle at various lengths anywhere from five feet or more from the bottom of the wall, so that means you must get a running start to propel yourself partially up the wall before you can even grab a rope to pull yourself up and over the Divide. Thank you, but no, thank you! I will stick to the side where the rope is touching the ground, and I can start climbing from there. However, my son and husband proceeded to the right side of the wall to run, jump, grab the rope, and climb. That left my daughter and me on the other side to get over the Divide by ourselves.

My adventurous daughter looked at me and said she would go first. She proceeded to climb the rope and got stuck, like I had in my two previous attempts, so she had to slide down to try again. She came back to me and said, "You try, Mom." So I did. I climbed the rope with more ease than before (this time, we had spent more time strength-training our upper bodies before the event), only to get stuck at my usual spot, just before the top, lying flat against the wall, hanging from that dang rope, so I had to slide down. I walked back to my daughter, and we watched as her brother and father made it up and over the top on the right side. We were happy for them, with a tinge of jealousy that they made it look so easy! We looked at each other and said, almost simultaneously, "Okay, let's give it another try."

This time, I went first. As I got to the top, to that spot that stops me, I questioned why in the world I was doing this in the first place! *What kind of crazy person am I? Do I need to prove anything to get over this beast? Will it really make a difference if I slide down and walk around?* All these thoughts were swirling in my head as I struggled to get to that chicken-wing spot at that top again. Then I heard in the background, "You got this, Mom!" And my heart grew ten times in that moment, giving me the strength to lift a sled over my head! Well, not really, but it was a Grinchy kind of moment—in a good way!

Now I replaced my thoughts of doubt with *I can't let her down. I've got to get over this so I can help HER do it. I CAN do this! I MUST do this!* It wasn't pretty, but I found the strength to swing my left leg up and over to where I was sideways on that thing at the top, and I could have easily rolled down the side I had just climbed up. Instead, I rolled to the point where I could straddle the top of the A-Frame and just sat there for a moment, absorbing my accomplishment and the incredible view. It was a beautiful view of the Tulsa area from the top of that A-Frame. I now understood why the curators placed this beast at the highest point: so if you did stop to take a moment to breathe in your accomplishment, you could look around and enjoy the view!

My daughter's cheers snapped me out of my moment of appreciation, and now my job was in front of me—my daughter would get over this Divide! I would make certain of it! She climbed up and was able to make it close enough to the top that I could reach her to help her over. Plus, a nice man had come up next to me and turned around to help me pull her over the top. Tackling that obstacle for myself is one thing but being able to turn around and help the next person, in this case, my daughter, is another thing altogether. I found "my purpose," that reason I needed to get over that beast that day. I had to get over to help my daughter; it wasn't only for or about me anymore. It was about her. Although, it didn't dawn on me how profound that was until we were rehashing the day's events on our way home that night.

There is power in your purpose

Your purpose or your why can sometimes be found in the most unlikely places. It might show up after you go through a workshop or a coaching session where you work through your vision of life and outline what matters most to you. Those exercises help you to identify your why or purpose when it is hard to nail down. Your answers could surprise you as you dig deeper into asking yourself why something is important to you and what you might accomplish should you proceed. Who might benefit, and where it could take you? Going through the process is extremely beneficial when you find yourself stuck in a rut or feel like you want to do something challenging.

   Other times, it might hit you as it did me that day on the wall. You replay some events in your head or with a partner or friend, and you realize why you did what you did. A sense of connection with your inner voice propelled you to act the way you did or to do something that truly aligned with your soul. For example: as I reflected on the wall, getting my daughter over it solidified how important my role as a mom and as a woman is for my daughter. I want her to know she can do anything she sets her mind to. And I want to be that role model for her that shows her not to give up, that it is okay to struggle and keep trying. I can say that I always knew that was my purpose as a mom, but I also know that I hadn't fully connected with this thought as deeply as I did at that moment on top of that wall. I connected with that something inside me that would enable me to move mountains for her if I needed to.

These moments are fleeting and can easily be overlooked. Taking note of these moments helps you to identify, and maybe even further solidify, what your purpose in life is. It will also energize you and keep you moving forward to meet whatever challenge is in front of you or accomplish whatever is important to you.

Another way to pull out your purpose is by journaling or working with a coach to connect with these inspiring moments to provide some insight into your purpose. Both give you the opportunity for reflection. When you journal your thoughts after or as you work through a challenge, try to extract your reason for taking on the challenge. Why did you want to take it on? What were you thinking when you started and when you hit bumps in the road? What are you working to accomplish? What benefit will it provide you or someone else? Does this align with your overall goals?

Working with a coach can help draw out these answers as well. Sometimes it is difficult to get through the echo in our heads. A coach hears what you are saying and can reflect your words. Even though you may have heard them in your head, hearing them in another person's voice has an impact. That impact provides reflection and can shine a light on what your true purpose is, helping you connect dots that you never connected before. Both of these methods are helpful when struggling to understand your purpose.

When you know your purpose, it helps you act with intention as you move through this life. Acting with intention is where you get your power because you now have alignment and focus. This pushes out your negative thoughts and moves you forward with positive momentum. Your purpose gives you the reason why you need to do that thing. And your reason why gives you the strength to do it.

Your purpose has an impact

Helping my daughter over the wall also made me realize how important it is for me to be mindful of my role as a parent. None of us are going to be perfect parents, and many times I joke that my children are going to go to therapy for something I did, I just don't know what it is at this moment. However, I think we forget at times how much we impact our children's lives. They are ALWAYS watching what we do and listening to what we say from infancy until they set out to tackle this big bad world on their own. Even then, they are watching and learning from us.

This thought helps me keep a clear head about the things I say and do around our children. I do my best to stay mindful of the examples we set and the time we spend together. Now that they are older, I realize how fleeting our time is with them and how much more important these OCRs have become for our family. Our son, who is now in college, comes home or meets us to take on these OCR challenges. They are another reason for us to get together as a family. Each time we go, we see how much our children have grown in their ability to take on life's challenges both on and off the field. Having such experiences with your children is truly priceless and will further serve you in finding your purpose or your why even after they leave the house.

Now, you might not choose to take on a mud run but finding family activities that might challenge you all will continue to increase the bond you have with your children as they set out on their own. You all may be scratching your head as to why you took something on, but when you do it as a family, those bonds become tighter because you are working toward a goal together.

The same can be said about you as a leader in your organization, no matter what title you hold. The people you work with, mentor, or report to, and your clients are all watching what you do. I think we tend to forget the impact we can have on others, positive or negative, in our daily lives. We will discuss this a bit more in the chapters on Collaboration. However, you may need to take a step back now and do some personal evaluation on why you are doing what you do in your job. Maybe it is for a certain cause as an organization. It might be to encourage those who follow you or to help a co-worker through a difficult task at the office or at home. Or maybe you work only to pay the bills.

Often, our work can get overwhelming, or maybe even underwhelming, and we question why we do it. At those moments, it is important to uncover why you are there—what is your purpose? You might not like the work, but the money you earn means you can support your family. Or there is another reason to do what you do. Discovering and understanding your purpose could make your day-to-day routine a little less monotonous. Or maybe highlight a need for a change.

We tackle tasks every day: things for our families, friends, jobs, and sometimes even ourselves. Without realizing it, you can lose sight of why you are doing these things. But every once in a while, you overcome something that has been haunting you, not because you needed to do it for yourself but because someone else is now counting on you to do it, and you are the role model for how they can accomplish it. That is one reason finding your purpose is so important.

Sometimes, the task must be about more than you, so you can find the strength to get through it.

Lesson

- Identify the obstacles you could take on but are avoiding
- Discover your purpose for doing so
- Understand your impact on others

Take Action

Describe a challenge you have been walking around even though you know you could accomplish it if you really needed to. Using the questions below, describe what it is, what your purpose is for overcoming it, and what benefit overcoming this obstacle will provide you and/or those around you.

Questions to Ponder

- What are you walking around or avoiding that you know, with a little more effort, you could accomplish?
- Is this something that you want to or need to overcome? If so, explain why and what it will take to overcome it.
- What actions do you need to take?
- Does accomplishing this serve your purpose for taking it on?
- What is that purpose?
- Is there a "why" that will help motivate you?
- How will it help others once you have accomplished it?

LESSONS FROM THE OBSTACLE COURSE

If you are still struggling with discovering why you need to accomplish this, then maybe it is something that you are not supposed to conquer. In the next chapter, we will discuss those obstacles in life that you don't need to take on.

5
PEGATRON

WHAT DO YOU NEED TO WALK AROUND?

*No one can win every battle,
but no one should fall without a struggle.*

—Peter Parker, *Spider-Man: Homecoming*

There are several difficult obstacles in these races. Not only are they mentally challenging, but they also require a significant amount of physical strength and training. People who are stronger and more agile than I can accomplish these obstacles, and I must admit that I am envious of them. I try to complete many of those challenges, only to get a few steps or rungs in before dropping into the pit of muddy water below.

One obstacle I attempt each time is the Stairway to Heaven, an upside-down V-shaped obstacle with slats of wood between the vertical posts that support it on each side which forms an "A" shape. It looks like an oversized ladder. However, you do not climb on the outside of this ladder as you would think. Instead, you climb on the inside and can only use your hands, no feet. As I have explained earlier, upper body strength is not my strong point. Plus, you need hand strength to hold on to the slats of wood that are worn down and slippery from all the muddy hands that have attempted to grasp them. To complete this obstacle, you must climb up one side, then turn around and climb down the other side, still on the inside of the ladder. If you cannot accomplish that, you end up dropping into the pit of muddy water below. That is where I end up. But I try each time, and each time, I get just a little further up the ladder.

The reason I keep trying is that one step further I get each time. I will most like never get through the entire obstacle, but I will keep trying to see how far I can get. I am okay if I do not complete it. I have learned to be okay with not conquering every challenge on the course. I can accept my limitations as long as I try my best.

Know when it's time to throw in the towel

One obstacle I am fine with not even attempting anymore is the Pegatron. This obstacle is a wall that has holes along its face, and it is sometimes suspended above yet another muddy water pit. The goal is to use pegs placed into the holes in the wall to maneuver your way across it. You can accomplish this obstacle by holding onto two pegs, one in each hand, and putting the pegs in the holes in the wall. To move across, you must take one peg out and put it in another hole as you hang from the other peg in the wall. You maneuver your way across the wall by hanging only onto the pegs as you alternate putting them in the holes. According to the Conquer the Gauntlet website, only about 19 percent of participants accomplish this feat. I can tell you I am not part of the 19 percent, and I am not even part of the maybe 50 percent who even attempt this obstacle. I simply walk around so that I can avoid another pit of muddy water.

At first, it bothered me to walk around the obstacle and not even try. I attempted it the first time and couldn't even get one peg out—it takes not just arm strength but total core, back, and hand strength to complete this task. It looks so cool when I see people get through it, and some make it look so easy! But it is not! And as much as I would like to find my internal Wonder Woman strength and get through that obstacle, it is not something I will ever be able to do. And that is okay.

Some obstacles are not worth the effort to complete or attempt. Being able to recognize this is crucial. You must set aside your pride to do so, though. How many tasks have you tried to power through because you had put so much into it already that you felt you had to do it, or you thought you would look bad for not doing it? But powering through only seems to make matters worse, or the job doesn't get done well. Or worse, you put yourself in a detrimental position. Sometimes we need to check our pride at the door and recognize when an obstacle or task is too much for us. We might not be prepared for it or don't have the skills, knowledge, training, time, or physical ability to do it.

Know the consequences

You must question if this is something you need to or want to do. On the Continental Divide, I knew I could get over it; I just had to try harder and have a reason to do so, which I eventually discovered was my daughter. As for Pegatron? Well, I have no internal or external reason I can tap into to answer why on Earth I should get across that thing. For a couple of reasons, it didn't matter to me if I made it through the obstacle. There was nothing for me to prove by accomplishing it. I had already set my pride aside, knowing that this one was beyond my ability. No one needed my help to get across it, so the only reason to do it was for myself. But I had no desire to complete it—it didn't matter to me. If they required burpees instead of the obstacle, which they do now, I gladly drop to complete them so I can move on to the next obstacle.

Many obstacles in life are the same. Sometimes, you should evaluate your reason for taking on the challenge. Why do you need to or want to accomplish this? If you did it but not as well as was necessary, what would happen? What would happen if you tried to get through the obstacle and failed? Would you face any consequences? Most importantly, does it matter if you take it on or not? If you cannot come up with a good reason to take on an obstacle, then you need to ask yourself what would happen if you did not address it. Can someone else who is more equipped than you take on this obstacle or task? Should they? If it needs to get done properly and you are not equipped to do that, is it better for all parties involved to leave it to someone else more capable? Our pride can trip us up with admitting that we cannot do something well, that someone else can, and then letting them do it. That can be a hard pill to swallow, but sometimes, we should.

Focus your efforts

Maybe it is something you could do, but it would be a waste of your time to do it or would take you longer to do it than someone else. Could someone else handle it for you so you can take on a bigger obstacle or task?

I am not saying that burpees are harder than crossing the Pegatron, but let's say for argument's sake that they are, and it would take me less time to do the burpees than to cross Pegatron. And something on the other side of this obstacle needed my attention. I know this is a stretch of the imagination but stick with me here. If this were the case, then I should do the burpees and let someone else who is more capable handle the Pegatron so I could get to the next obstacle or task sooner. Dividing and conquering the tasks that we are more capable of doing is a better use of our skill sets, allowing for both the obstacle and the task to be accomplished in a timely manner.

It is imperative that we don't allow pride to keep us from recognizing when we cannot (or should not) do something because we do not have the ability to do it. We also need to recognize when it is time to let someone else take on the obstacle or task so we can address other ones that are within our wheelhouse or are no longer a good use of our time and efforts.

Know where you want to go

Another reason to recognize when it is time to walk around an obstacle or challenge in life is that your efforts are not taking you where you want or need to be. We often set up expectations and goals that are not our own or they are no longer relevant. Yet, we spend countless hours and enormous energy trying to overcome them. It could be a job, relationship, personal goal, or any number of things that you once thought were worthwhile, but it has now become an energy and time drain.

Walking around or away might be difficult because you have invested so much into the task. Or it may feel like you failed if you do not stick with it and prevail. But is it worth it? What will you gain by doing so? What would you gain by walking around it? I am not saying you should give up without attempting the obstacle or challenge unless you have no reason to do so, but sometimes you must evaluate whether or not the task is worth completing.

That does not mean you should not take on difficult challenges. Rather, you should pause and think about the challenge from another viewpoint. Take some time to evaluate whether the obstacle is still worth overcoming. If it is, then maybe you need more training or skill to accomplish it. In the case of Pegatron, if I wanted to overcome it, I would put up the peg board my husband made, then engage in a training and skills program so I could accomplish my goal. I would need to put more thought into my workout schedule and add more core, upper body, and hand strength training, along with adjusting my routine. However, as I mentioned, I have no desire to do so, and no one needs me to get across this thing so that I can help them. Therefore, there is no need for me to put in such effort and no reason to endure all that pain.

Don't walk away because it is too hard

A word of caution here, though! Before you drop a relationship, job, or any other obstacle that is too challenging for you now, you should do some soul-searching and ask yourself some serious questions. Walking away from something because it is too hard or challenging is not the right thing to do. Ever. You must put in the hard work and endure the pain to accomplish some things in life that matter to you or those you love. And even some that don't matter to you but do need to get done.

Take the time to evaluate and recognize the difference between what is worth it and what is not. I touched on one important reason not to walk away before evaluating an obstacle when I mentioned no one needed me to complete the Pegatron obstacle. I was not letting anyone down, and no one was relying on me to complete it. If someone were, I would have approached the obstacle with a different mindset.

As it is, I can walk away knowing that I am the only one that this will impact.

If the obstacle is one that the team (work or family team) needs to complete, then you need to evaluate how best to get it done. Do you enlist help, as mentioned above? Do you train harder or develop another skill set? What are the consequences if you walk away from or around the obstacle in your path? This can be a significant question for you, especially if you are evaluating a job or a relationship. If that is the case, it might be helpful to break down the situation into smaller obstacles and evaluate each one separately before you decide to walk around. Or enlist the help of others in evaluating your situation, making certain this is one you no longer need to stick with or take on.

Live to Fight Another Day

As for Pegatron and this part of Discovery, the key issues are to recognize when it is time to walk around an obstacle and know it is okay to do so. Often, you need to conserve your energy for the obstacles you must face and overcome and not feel bad about those you walked around or away from. If you know when it is time to give up the fight so you can fight another day, it can help you stop wasting time and energy on obstacles you do not need or desire to overcome. Most importantly, it will give you the peace of mind that it is okay to move on with no regrets.

Lesson

- Identify the obstacles you do not need to take on
- Decide where you should focus your efforts
- Don't let pride get in the way

Take Action

Describe a challenge you have been facing that you think you need to walk around. Using the questions below, describe what it is, why you feel you should not take this on, and what is keeping you from doing so.

Questions to Ponder:

- Why do you need to accomplish this?
- What would happen if you did not?
- What would happen if you did, but not as well as it needed to get done?
- What would happen if you tried to get through the obstacle and failed?
- What consequences would you face? Most importantly, does it matter?
- What happens when you do not take it on or you leave it to someone else to do?
- Can someone else who is more equipped than you take on this obstacle/task? Should they?
- Could someone else handle it for you so you can take on a bigger obstacle/task?
- What will you, or others, gain by doing so?

Now that you have found your purpose for overcoming challenging obstacles and you have discovered which ones you need to walk away from, let's tackle those yucky ones that just need to get done.

6

THE SEWER AND UP FROM THE GRAVE

ARE YOU AFRAID TO GET MESSY?

You're much stronger than you think you are. Trust me.

—Superman, *Superman*

The muddy and slightly disturbing obstacles in these OCR courses were something I didn't expect would add to my personal growth. Yet they did and in surprising ways! These are the ones that make you wince when you get to them and say to yourself, *Really? I have to do what now?* In Conquer the Gauntlet, a few obstacle names not only make you think twice about them, leaving you scratching your head and wondering why you even signed up for the race in the first place, but the mere sight of them makes you question your sanity. The Sewer and Up from the Grave are just a couple of examples of these obstacle head-scratchers.

First Things First

These obstacles are easy to do from a physical standpoint, but you must plug your nose to get through them! Quite literally! Some obstacles cause you to check a few worries at the door and just dive in. One such obstacle is the Sewer.

The Sewer is a large pipe you must climb through while muddy water also runs through it. It reminds me of the big cement pipes you find under bridges and roads that you might have explored as a kid, hence the name. However, even as kids, we knew to avoid the ones with water or mud running through them. Who would want to get that dirty? Now, as an adult, I pay someone so I can get that dirty. Sometimes I truly do wonder about my sanity.

The space is tight in the Sewer, and it gets a little dark because it is a long, black tube. If you are claustrophobic, crawling through that thing can add more to the self-challenge. It is not difficult, only dark, dank, dirty, and a little stinky. Like many obstacles or tasks in life, it is one you simply must do. I don't even want to say power through because you need no extra physical effort since you only crawl through it to get to the other side. Although, you might have to overcome some psychological barriers to complete it. You could walk around it, but if the physical effort is minimal, why wouldn't you at least give it a try?

Tackling the Sewer is like tackling that task you must do but don't want to. Many call it eating the frog or first things first. They mean that if you tackle the projects or tasks you dislike first or head-on, you make progress because you get them out of the way and don't need to think about them anymore. Much like plugging your nose or more like holding your breath as you crawl through the Sewer. You just need to do it and do it as quickly as possible so you can get it out of the way. When you get these tasks out of the way first thing or as quickly as you can, then they are done, and you do not need to worry about them until they come up again. That is easier said than done sometimes because none of us really want to do the things that we do not enjoy. But you need to.

TRUST YOURSELF

We also dislike things that seem more challenging, bigger, or scarier than they are. Up from the Grave fits that description.

When you come to this obstacle, you truly start to question your sanity. It looks like a row of toilets in the ground, or at least that is what I thought when I first encountered this little gem of an obstacle. Picture a platform of several large dark holes approximately two feet in diameter, made from about four or five feet of black tubing that dumps straight down into another pit of muddy water. However, you cannot see the bottom of the tube because the dirty water comes right up to the bottom of it. The intent is for you to drop yourself into the tube, hoping to hit the bottom, then swim underneath the end of the tube and come out the other side in the pit of murky water. If you thought the Sewer was worrisome, you would love this one.

As with the Sewer, it is not all that physically challenging. Instead, it is a mental game. Are you willing to drop yourself through the tube into the murky water below and dunk your head in so you can swim out the other side? It entails trust—trust you will find the bottom, can swim under the tube, and will come out the other side unharmed. Also, you must trust in yourself.

When you put your trust in a system, you may doubt whether it will work. Watching others will help. If they make it out the other side, then you should be able to as well. It involves trusting yourself, too, because you must willingly dunk your head in and swim out. Are you able to trust yourself not to panic and make matters worse? Can you see yourself completing the task? It doesn't mean you have to complete the task with perfection. You only need to get through the task at hand. Can you envision yourself getting through to the other side? Can you trust your ability to do so? Being able to trust yourself and the process is part of the mental game. If you can embrace that, then you can get through the obstacle, so long as the yucky part doesn't stop you.

To force yourself to face the yuck in any task is challenging. Yet when you do, there is a sense of accomplishment in that you could face the yuck and still prevail.

Many things in life are just yucky, but you still need to do them. It could be a task your boss requests or something your family needs, like changing diapers or cleaning up dog puke. Really it doesn't get any yuckier than that! Yet it must be done, plain and simple. If you trust yourself, then you can get through the process, prevail, and come out the other side relatively unscathed. The only thing left to do is dig in and get dirty. You will not get hurt, and you can always clean up.

Keep perspective

The amazing thing about facing the yuck is that when you look back on it after you completed it, you realize it wasn't as bad as you thought it would be. The task wasn't that hard, the effort was minimal, and the yuck wasn't as yucky as you had imagined. Often, our imaginations make things scarier and tougher than they are.

Another key component of the mental game is to control your thoughts. Sometimes watching others accomplish the task is helpful. With the Up from the Grave, watching others prevail provided the assurance that there was a bottom at the end of this tube and that I could quickly dunk in and swim out the other side unharmed.

Other than watching others complete a worrisome task, you can discuss it with someone who has done it before and can shed the necessary light to make it less scary. What a great help it is to have a mentor or a friend, someone who has walked the path you are about to embark on and can provide some guidance or assurance that you have it in you to accomplish whatever you want to do. Regardless of how you get through the yucky horrible task, you will find strength in knowing you can accomplish it with few to no issues and put it behind you. That is until the dog pukes again.

Be the leader

One thing to remember about getting through the yuck yourself is that once you do so, you become the leader, the example, the one to help others get through and face their yucky demons. An example of this is in the final mud pit in the Warrior Dash. This race has a few muddy obstacles scattered throughout the course as well, but none as muddy as the last one. This last obstacle is literally a mud pit about twenty feet long. To get to the finish line and collect your bling, you must crawl through the mud on your belly since you have to go under the barbed wire that hangs over the pit.

The kids had fun with this one on their second race. On their first race, however, it did not thrill them that this was the final obstacle they had to maneuver through. Watching them do it was entertaining for us as parents, but it was also a proud-parent moment to witness them face something gross, and with a little complaining, get through it.

When we first arrived at the pit, the kids looked at my husband and me with an expression that said, *"Are you serious? We have to go through that?"* Even though they had seen me complete the last mud pit in my first obstacle-course race a couple of years before, doing it themselves was entirely different. We wouldn't let them walk around it, though. Instead, we assured them it was only mud, and they would be all right.

I have a great picture of our daughter with a pirate look on her face as she winced when the person in front of her kicked mud into her face. The photo of our son shows a look of pure disgust. I still giggle each time I see those pictures. But like the troopers they are, they faced the challenge of the muddy pit and prevailed! That meant they faced their fear of and displeasure with getting so filthy that mud covered every inch of their bodies. I mean, it is *everywhere*! Plus, since we wouldn't let them walk around the obstacle, they had to face it. Part of being a parent is teaching your kids that it is not a legitimate excuse to refuse a task or challenge because it is difficult or messy. Setting the example and not letting them off the hook has done amazing things for our kids' mental and physical growth.

The second time they did that course, they had so much more fun with the muddy pit because they had already done it and realized it was only mud, and the pit could be fun without their fear or repulsion. We encouraged the kids to bring a friend on their second encounter with the Warrior Dash. My son and his friend literally dove into the pit, covering themselves from head to toe with mud. I have a great picture of them, which we now refer to as the mud-men group, not the Blue Man Group, where you can only see their eyes because of the mud. My daughter laughed as her friend, new to this obstacle course experience, had the same look on her face that our daughter had in her first race—the "Are you kidding me?" look. We had so much fun watching them encourage and support their friends through this last pit! It was another proud-parent moment!

Pushing through the mental, not physical, challenges of these courses has taught me a lot about what I am made of inside and to not be afraid of getting a little dirty. That means diving into a yucky task and getting it done. I still dislike doing some things, but once they are done and out of the way, I feel so much better because it means I can move on to do something else. Check the box, cross it off your list, or do whatever motivates you to complete the task. And feel good knowing that you faced the yuck and prevailed.

Lesson

- Identify the yucky tasks that you don't want to do but need to
- Discover ways to take them on to get past them
- Be an example to others

Take Action

Describe a challenge you have been avoiding, something that you really do not want to do because it is yucky. Once you describe what it is, think about what you feel is holding you back and what you think it will take for you to accomplish this obstacle/challenge in your life and put it behind you.

Questions to Ponder

- What tasks are you avoiding because they are just dirty, yucky tasks to do?
- How will you feel when you get them done?
- What is it about this task/obstacle that you do not like?
- Will it harm you?
- Is it more of a mental challenge for you? Or a physical (skill set) challenge?

- Do you trust yourself to get through it? Why or why not?
- What is worrying you about this task?
- What is the worst thing that can happen if you take it on?
- Do you need some help or guidance because you have not done it before? If yes, who could help you?
- Who can you help if you get through this task?
- What would happen if you didn't complete this challenge? Who is relying on you to get this done?

Now that we have discovered your purpose for taking on difficult obstacles and discussed the ones you need to walk away from and the yucky ones you just need to do, let's get into some strategies to help you persist through the challenges you face.

PART 3
Persistency

7

CONQUERORS CARRY

HOW DO YOU GO ON DESPITE THE LOAD YOU CARRY?

It's not who I am underneath, but what I do that defines me.

—Bruce Wayne/Batman, *Batman Begins*

Now that we have shed some light on what you are recovering from and you have some ideas on how to go through the Discovery process, let's dive into Persistency. Some call this grit, powering through, or *just do it*® as the famous Nike® slogan has encouraged us all to do. But what does that really mean to you? What burdens are you carrying with you that make it more challenging to grit your teeth and power through? What lessons can you take away from the obstacle course that will help you here?

Besides the length of some of these courses (some are up to twenty-plus miles), there is always an obstacle or two that is difficult to complete but doable. These obstacles require the ability to dig deep and persist through the challenge at hand. The obstacle that reflects this challenge well in the Conquer the Gauntlet race is called the Conquerors Carry.

The challenge is to carry a fifty-pound bag of sand over a long stretch of the course without putting it down and leaving it behind. When we did this one in Tulsa, Oklahoma, in 2016 and 2018, the obstacle began and ended at the top of a big hill. Which meant you picked up the fifty-pound bag at the top of the hill, carried it down, then back up the hill again before you could drop it off and be on your way to the next obstacle. To add insult to injury, the trail was not straight down or up. No, that might have made things a little easier. Instead, the trail meandered down and back up the hill, as you would find if you hiked in the mountains. A single-track trail with rocks, tree trunks, and some steep sides. So you not only had to balance the fifty-pound sack you were carrying, but you also had to find your balance as you navigated the trail.

Persisting through the challenge

I don't know how long the trail was, maybe about a quarter of a mile, but regardless of the length, it was challenging. The first challenge is figuring out how to position the fifty-pound bag you must carry. I saw people holding it like a baby in their arms, carrying it on one shoulder with one arm, and others carrying it on their hips. Not to say one way is better than another; each person must figure out the best way to carry their own load for the duration of this obstacle, just as they do in life. We will return to that thought in a bit. For me, I found that slinging this fifty-pound bag of sand over my head to get it balanced on my shoulders, neck, and upper back was the most comfortable way for me to distribute and carry this load. With the bag in position, I began my way down the trail.

Going down the hill wasn't too bad. I had to manage my balance and the tendency to go too fast and fall forward. Gravity wanted to propel me and the weight I was carrying down the hill at a speed faster than I wanted to go. A few people passed me as they jogged down the hill with the weight on their shoulders. I said a few kind words of encouragement and celebration out loud and a few not-so-kind words under my breath as they jogged past me. Okay, a little competition and jealousy creep in sometimes; I'm only human. Also, a few people came a little too close for comfort as I tried to balance myself and my load on the single-track, causing me to struggle to regain my composure. Once at the bottom, I faced going back up the hill. My legs, specifically my quads, felt weak because they had worked hard to keep me from going down the hill too fast. Now they had to work differently, along with my glutes, to push me and the extra weight back up the hill.

As I slowly climbed the hill, it was a pleasant surprise to see that I was the one now passing a few people on the trail and some sitting on the side to catch their breath. My single thought, though, on my uphill climb, was that I wouldn't stop. I thought if I stopped, it would be too hard to get going again. So I put my head down, focused on the trail, and kept walking. I occasionally stole a glimpse at the top of the hill to see how much farther I had to go, but for most of the walk, I kept my head down and focused on the next step.

There was a cartoon I watched when I was a kid where the female character chanted, "NACI," which is "I can" backward. She did this when she had an obstacle to overcome and needed encouragement to complete the task. Saying "I can" backward was her mantra. I chant this when the task is long and hard. It is now my mantra when training for longer running events, such as half-marathons, or even when the one minute of the HIIT (High-Intensity Interval Training) or a weight training workout seems to drag on forever. When the road gets long, and I get tired, I start chanting "NACI" under my breath or in my mind. It gives me something to focus on besides the pain in my body, and it gives me the mental courage to continue. I CAN do this.

For this climb, I not only needed to find a place for my mind to go when my legs and lungs started screaming at me, which is where my "NACI" mantra came in, but I also had to dig deep and focus on the next step only. If I kept my focus on the top of the hill, it would have discouraged me because it was a very steep hill, and the top was really far away. By keeping my focus on the next step in front of me, maintaining my momentum, and resisting the urge to stop and rest, I made it to the top without putting the bag down or stopping. Persistence is about doing just that—putting your head down and continuing through the task, no matter how hard it is or the burden you carry.

THE LOAD YOU CARRY

For that obstacle and Persistency, it is not only about powering through the challenge itself, but it is also about handling the load you are carrying while you are persisting through the obstacle. That happens in life too. It is never just the task that you must manage, but other things you must contend with that are making the task much more difficult than it would be on its own. If I only had to walk or jog the hiking trail down and up the hill, that wouldn't be so bad. But doing it while carrying a fifty-pound bag—which is about 30 percent to 40 percent of my body weight, depending on the year, well that adds a whole other aspect to this challenge, which also mirrors what happens in life.

If we could take on one thing at a time always, I think we would all be more successful. But life is not that easy. Every day, we must balance something as we work to accomplish any task. It could be our children, finances, work, family, health, personal demons, and the list goes on. It is how we handle this load when tackling an obstacle that will make a difference in how well we navigate and ultimately succeed at the challenge.

First, you must discover how to best balance or manage your load. As I mentioned earlier, each person picked up and held that fifty-pound bag differently. Some held it in their arms like a baby, which for me would be too difficult to do for long because it would take much more effort than my arms could endure. Plus, exhausting my arms on this obstacle would make it more difficult for me to complete the other obstacles on the course. Not holding the bag in my arms meant I would have more energy to take on the other remaining obstacles on the course that day.

Others held the bag on one shoulder with one arm. That would be more doable for me, but not for long, and meant I would need to shift shoulders periodically. Shifting the load would break my mental focus, which would cause me more delay or possibly force me to stop and pause, which is not what I wanted to do on that hill. I wanted the hill to be over with as quickly as possible, so balancing that fifty-pound bag without disrupting my focus was important to my overall success with the obstacle.

Find Your Way

I could go through all the other ways people carried their load, but I think you get the point. You must carry your burdens as best suits you. Trial and error will help, but it also takes knowing yourself, what you can manage, and what you need to overcome those difficult life tasks or obstacles you will face. You discover what works best for you by evaluating a situation while or after you go through it. Also, if you are fortunate enough to know others who are managing the same challenge, observe how they do it, or discuss it with those who have already completed the task.

Keep analyzing and monitoring how you feel. Soon you will find what suits you best. And it doesn't matter if it looks odd or uncomfortable to others. So long as it suits you and you are comfortable, that is all that matters. You are the one who must carry it, not someone else.

The first time we did Conquerors Carry, we were lucky enough not to have to navigate a hill, but we still had to carry the same fifty-pound bag. This first time through, I tried the one-shoulder technique; that is why I knew I would have to shift the weight from shoulder to shoulder during the trek. On that course, I watched how others managed their load, and by the end of the walk, I had the bag squarely positioned on my shoulders, neck, and back, where the weight was much more manageable for me. It wasn't all that comfortable, but it was doable.

You do the same thing as you manage your burdens in life. Sometimes you may find you need the help of support groups or friends to figure out how best to manage the burden you are carrying. Others who have gone through the same issue you are now facing. Knowing that you do not need to face a challenge on your own but can rely on how others managed through can take some of the stress off of you as you complete the challenge in front of you. They can give you ideas and insight on how to manage the burden you are carrying. Or they are there to support you mentally as you move through the task before you.

But ultimately, it is your decision on how best to manage your load. You are the only one who knows what you can truly manage. Knowing yourself and watching others gives you the insight to help you figure that out.

Lessons from the Obstacle Course

Where You Focus Matters

Sometimes there are tasks in life that you must power through. To do so, you must focus so you can persist through the task at hand while you carry your load or burden. Some common principles are helpful, and chances are you have heard these before. You should focus on your next best step (as I did when I climbed the hill), not on how far you still must go. Because when you focus on how far you still must go, it discourages you. Instead, when you look at how far you have already come, it encourages you to persist. That's what worked for me on the Conquerors Carry hill.

I found that if I focused on the top of the hill, I was discouraged because of how far I still had to go. By looking down at my feet and my next step, I could steal a glimpse behind me at the bottom of that big hill, slowly watching it get farther in the distance. That gave me encouragement that I was making progress, which was the exact thing I needed.

I have heard this same analogy in the metaphor of climbing the staircase. Your goal is at the top of the staircase. But if you keep your focus on the goal, the top of the stairs, you miss out on the little things, and it can discourage you because you are focusing on how far you still must go instead of the next task or next step to get you there.

When you have an enormous task in front of you, focusing on the end can make it look even bigger than it is, which will make the task much more daunting than it is. When something seems large and insurmountable, we are more likely to get discouraged, not persist, and give up. If you need to complete a really big goal, then that is the last thing you want to do. Instead, if you focus on the next task of the big goal, you can keep your momentum going because small, consistent successes over time lead you to your end goal.

It is good to know where your end goal is and keep it in mind so you stay on track. That means checking in with the goal periodically to make sure it is still where you want and need to go, as I did by occasionally looking up to see how much farther I had to go up that hill. However, it doesn't help when you keep focusing on it. Besides discouraging you and draining your energy, you will miss out on the little wins along the way if you don't pay attention to the smaller steps that get you to your goal. This brings me to the other reason it is important to focus on your next step instead of the end goal.

THE LITTLE THINGS

Taking the hill one step at a time helped me stay consistent with my trek up and allowed me to see what was going on around me as I climbed. When I passed other people, I noticed I didn't breeze by them with a single-minded focus on getting to the top. Instead, I appreciated that I could pass them, had the strength and fortitude in my resolve to conquer this hill without stopping, was managing my fifty-pound burden well, and that my training had paid off, giving me the strength to make it up this hill. I smiled and encouraged them as I passed as well, with the hope that by showing them I could make it to the top, they could too.

I know it might sound odd, but I enjoyed the battle of the hill because I had conquered the battle in my mind and body. Passing others who had stopped helped me to appreciate my accomplishment even more. If I had stayed focused on the top, the end goal only, I would have missed that. I also think I couldn't have appreciated it because my focus on how far I still had to go would have discouraged me.

I have always liked Miley Cyrus's song "The Climb," and I think the chorus of that song sums it up beautifully when she says it isn't about the speed at which she gets to the top; it is the climb to get there that matters.

LESSONS FROM THE OBSTACLE COURSE

Goals will always be there, whether they are yours or something you must do for your job or your family; you will always have something you need to strive for. Some you will enjoy, some you will not, but you must accomplish them. And you will also have burdens you need to carry along the way. It will be up to you to figure out how best to manage them to accomplish your goals while carrying your fifty-pound bag.

Most importantly, though, don't forget to enjoy the moments and the little wins along the way.

Don't forget to enjoy the climb!

Lesson

- Identify how you persist through tough challenges
- Understand what loads you are carrying
- Break down large goals into manageable, bite-sized pieces

Take Action

Is there a goal that you need to accomplish that seems insurmountable? What burdens are you carrying with you while you set out to accomplish this goal? Once you have identified what the goal is and the burdens you are carrying with you, go through the following questions.

Questions to Ponder

- Can you break down the goal into smaller tasks?
- What are your wins along the way?
- How will you check in to see how much farther you need to go and if you are still on track for reaching your goal?

- How will you check in with yourself to see how far you have come?
- How are you carrying your load?
- Is it balanced for you?
- Do you need to shift it any?
- Has someone else (person, book, podcast, etc.) walked this path that you can get ideas from?
- Do you have a mantra or something you can focus on?
- How do you stay focused when you need to stay on task?

Sometimes it is not the burdens that stop us from completing a challenge—it is our fears. Next, we will discuss how you overcome the evil demons lurking in the darkness of your mind.

8

ROCKIES

What do you fear?

I can't control their fear, only my own.

—Wanda Maximoff, *Captain America: Civil War*

A surprising lesson from the OCR courses was the fear that I faced at times was not the fear of failure. It was my fear of getting hurt or injured. It differed from fear of failure, or maybe it is part of it. On these courses, I do not care if I fail at an obstacle so long as I have attempted it. Where I get frustrated with myself is when I do not attempt it because I am afraid that I will fall and get hurt. I have mentioned this a few times in previous chapters, so let's unpack this a bit more and look at why it is important, not just on the course, but in life.

The Rockies was one of those challenges that I knew I could do but didn't try because I imagined myself getting hurt doing so. Instead of tackling it, I walked around it that first time through, using Frank's injured arm as my excuse. Walking around it bothered me because my fear of getting hurt surprised me. I didn't anticipate that fear would hold me back from taking on obstacles that were relatively easy to do.

This obstacle is a series of three angled walls in a row. They are not too high but high enough and angled enough that you need to get a little momentum going so you can jump up, grab the top and pull yourself over. The first one is not so bad because you have the space to get a running start to give yourself enough momentum to run, walk up, or bear-climb the wall to grab the top and pull yourself over. The next two walls are closer together, so you need to rely more on strength, speed, or a friend at the top to propel you far enough up the angled wall to reach for the top and work your way over.

My fear wasn't that I wouldn't have enough momentum to get myself far enough up the wall to grab the top to climb over. I feared I would end up lying flat against the wall, as I did on the Continental Divide wall, not able to pull myself over or that I would come down hard on my knees as I attempted to propel myself up and over the wall.

That fear kept me from taking on the obstacle the first time I encountered it. The fear made me mad at myself when I got home and realized I could have gotten over those walls. Especially if 92 percent of participants, per their website, can conquer the task. With such a high success percentage, why did I give up on myself? Why didn't I at least try to get over those walls? What was holding me back? Those walls haunted me because I let my fear of getting hurt stop me from doing something I knew I could do.

How fear holds us back

There are several reasons why we do not take on an obstacle or a difficult task in life. We might be afraid of getting hurt or looking bad because we are taking on something new, and the outcome is unknown. We might even doubt our ability because we have never done it before. We might be stretching ourselves beyond our known capabilities. This happens whether it is a physical obstacle, one at work, or in our personal lives.

Fear of getting hurt can be debilitating and cut us off at the knees. It can make us stay too long in one place where we shouldn't or not take on something new that we know we should. To face our fear and move beyond it, we must look at why we are afraid. What is it that scares us? If this thing that scares us happens, how bad will it really be? Is it something we can recover from? Is the hurt we fear going to be as bad as we imagine?

In facing the Rockies, I pictured myself slamming down against those walls and bruising my knees. I also pictured myself scraping my arms as I attempted to pull myself over the top. None of those injuries would have been major or would stop me from completing the other obstacles on the course, but for some reason, that day when I first encountered those walls, the fear of those things was enough to stop me from climbing the walls. Not that I didn't have the confidence in my ability to climb them, but it was the thought of getting hurt that kept me from taking them on.

As human beings, we tend to think the worst is going to happen—our monkey brains stick the tape, CD, or YouTube video on replay in our minds. Often, we think bad things will happen based on past unpleasant experiences. We play back the loop several times in our minds, reminding us of why we failed, the feelings we had when it happened, and why we shouldn't or cannot try again. Or if we venture into something new that stretches or challenges us, that we will fail again as we did in the past and get hurt. By the time we have heard this loop a thousand times, we believe it, even if it is not true.

To break through that fear, we must break the loop or insert something else into the loop that changes the outcome. Instead of telling yourself that you cannot do something, tell yourself you can. This isn't something new or groundbreaking; I am sure you have heard this before. However, as much as we know something, it takes a while to apply it.

We also have an instinctive caution that keeps us from doing things that make us uncomfortable or might harm us. This is our primitive brain keeping us safe and out of danger. It was why our species has lived so long. If a bear growls in the woods, it is probably a smart thing to run from it, not toward it. Keeping us safe from harm is an instinct.

If the fear we have from our experiences doesn't stop us, the fear of the unknown does. What will happen if we try something different or new that stretches us beyond our current abilities or that challenges us or the status quo? When we face an obstacle in life that brings up this fear, we do one of three things: fight, flight, or freeze.

In our first race, I was telling myself I would get hurt if I attempted to do some of the simple obstacles that I knew I could do. That commentary in my brain made me run (flight) from them. Well, I didn't really run screaming in fright from the obstacles, but I did walk around many instead of facing them. The fear of getting hurt caught me off guard. I grew up climbing trees; why would I fear a few bruises or scrapes? I don't intend to discount the serious injuries that can happen on these courses. However, if you push yourself to do a physical activity that you have not done before or that is challenging, then it comes with the expectation that you could get hurt.

And that is the point here. They design these races to challenge you, to push you beyond what you think you can do. In doing so, chances are you will get a little banged up. Those can be badges of honor! As in life, any challenge can bang you up. Nothing will be perfect or smooth. If it were, I am not sure it would be worth doing. It is the struggle that makes the win so enjoyable and keeps us coming back for more, so we can struggle to win or at least conquer the task to know that we accomplished something challenging in our lives.

Larger than life

As if the fear of getting hurt wasn't enough for our imagination to make us run for the hills, the other crazy thing we do to ourselves is worry that the outcome of attempting a challenge could be worse than it is. We imagine things are bigger than they are, that the cute little kitten in front of us is now a ferocious lion who hasn't eaten in three weeks.

Our imaginations are wonderful things that can work for us or against us. I imagined I would slam down so hard on those walls that it would hurt like heck, and I would be limping through the rest of the race. Really I did! Although I know that wasn't a true risk, my thoughts convinced me it was. I did the same thing with a few other obstacles that day, and I took on a few that I really should have worried about but didn't. My only explanation for this is that after my run-in with the giant wall, these little walls became much larger in my mind than they were. I let my experience of attempting and failing to climb over the big one influence my resolve to take on these little walls. Instead of seeing myself getting over them, I saw myself getting hurt.

That is how other things can influence our perception of how well we can overcome an obstacle. It is tempting and easy to let negative experiences with some obstacles in life taint how we perceive similar ones. How one failure can lead to future failures because we believe we will fail at similar challenges. Such repetitive thoughts lead us to envision the same outcome in other experiences or obstacles. Seeing a different outcome is challenging, even if the circumstances, players, relationships, or situations are different. If there are enough similarities, the playback in our minds tells us the outcomes will be similar. Our minds keep telling us: *Don't go there. If you do, you will get hurt, you will fail, and the outcome will be the same—danger*! But will it? You won't know until you try. Mustering the guts to try again is the hard part. But you must, or you will never know if you can conquer the obstacle.

MANAGE YOUR EXCUSES

There was one more thing that enabled me to give in to my fear that day. This was our first race together, the one that Frank got hurt in. So I reasoned it was okay not to face my fear because Frank couldn't get over the walls, either. He became my excuse, the way I let myself off the hook that day for several obstacles I could have conquered. As I look back, it's interesting that the obstacles for which I used Frank as my excuse for avoiding were the ones I could have taken on by myself. I would have struggled, but I could have done them. I chose not to, though. That is why I felt disappointed in myself later and decided I wouldn't let that happen again.

The decision to not let someone else influence whether you accept a scary challenge is not as easy as it sounds. We may not know it, but if we are honest, I bet we can find several times when we chose not to do something because a friend, colleague, spouse, or someone else wasn't doing it or had influenced our decision somehow.

I recall in high school when a friend of mine and I tried out for the basketball team. I enjoyed the practices and thought I had a slight chance of making the team. My friend, however, didn't like the practices and dropped out. Because she wasn't there and I didn't know anyone else on the team, I dropped out too. I also know I was worried that I wouldn't make the team, which would have hurt and was the main reason I let my friend's decision influence me to drop out. If she weren't there and I didn't know anyone, well, it wouldn't be as much fun, right? I wish now that I hadn't dropped out, that I had stayed on and had seen it through. I will never know the potential outcome of staying, but I can use my curiosity about the possibilities to remind me not to give up on trying something new and challenging.

No regrets

Occasionally, I do forget this life lesson. It is easier sometimes to have a good excuse not to try something new and challenging. But that is not a good reason not to try; life is too short, and each day, it is getting shorter. As I get older, that thought propels me even more to try the things that scare me and not let my worry about getting hurt or others' influence determine whether I attempt a challenge. When I look back on my life as an old lady in a rocking chair, I want to have very few regrets. That means I need to face my fears. That dang clock is ticking!

When we encountered these walls in future races, I am happy to say I overcame my fear and the walls! They were not as big as I imagined them to be. I did fall on my knee on one of them, and I did scrape my arms going over the top of them. Bruised, yes, but they did no actual damage. I prevailed! Best of all, they are puny little walls in my mind now! I laugh, thinking that they even bothered me in the first place. I know there will be more walls to climb, and with these behind me, I am ready to take them on!

Always remember that, most likely, the worst thing you imagine will happen will not, but the regret you will feel for not trying will stay with you for a very long time. If it is worth doing, if it is something you want to take on or overcome, don't you want to be able to look back on your life and say you had the guts to do it?

Live life with no regrets!

Lesson

- Identify what fears hold you back
- Keep proper perspective
- Manage your excuses

Take Action

What do you need to take on that has been haunting you? That you know you could conquer if you just tried, but you have let your fear hold you back. Is it truly a big scary lion, or is it a kitten? Use the questions below to help you analyze this situation and others you might have not taken on.

Questions to Ponder

- What is the challenge?
- What is holding you back?
- What past experiences are similar to the one before you?
- What other influences are affecting your decision to face the challenge?
- What would happen if you did?
- What would happen if you don't?
- Is this really a lion or a cute little kitten?
- What do you see happening when you take on this challenge?

LESSONS FROM THE OBSTACLE COURSE

- Will you really get hurt if you face this obstacle?
- If you do get hurt, how bad would it really be?

After you have your steps written down for taking on a big obstacle and you have the proper perspective on how difficult it will be, the last thing to do is to power through it. Easier said than done, though. Next, we will discuss some strategies you can consider.

9

BOARD CRAWL

WHAT PUSHES YOU FORWARD?

Don't ever tell me there's no way.

—Phil Coulson, *Agents of S.H.I.E.L.D.*

I am not too sure what this obstacle was called because it is no longer on the Conquer the Gauntlet website. So, I will call it the Board Crawl because that is what I did to get across it. This obstacle was the one that made me fall in love with obstacle course races because it challenged me in so many ways, and I completed it on my terms. Not exactly how I was supposed to complete it if I were competing, but I made it to the other side without falling into the muddy water pit below. I call that a success!

We encountered it on our first obstacle course race in Little Rock, Arkansas, in 2015. We were about two-thirds of the way through the course when we came to this obstacle. Frank had already hurt his arm, so he was completing the obstacles he could, passing on the ones he couldn't. Due to his arm, he could not take on the Board Crawl. Even though he didn't do it, he stayed right there with me as I did, guiding me and cheering me on.

You could compare this obstacle's setup to that of an unfinished deck. It is a series of boards that span across a pit of muddy water below. The structure looks like the underside of a raised deck without the deck boards, just the joists that would support the future deck. This obstacle comprises several boards for you to take your pick from to get across since each one spans the length of the pit. Your challenge, should you accept it, is to hang from the board over the water and work your way to the other side. For the competitive round, they allow participants to only use their hands to go across the board. Like Pegatron and a few other obstacles, you need upper body and hand strength to get across those boards. Since I was not there to compete, nor did I have the upper body and hand strength to take me across this board in the manner the competitors would, I had to find another way if I were to take on this obstacle.

Watch for inspiration

As we approached, I watched others trying to get across. Many did the hand-over-hand technique of crossing the board. Some made it, but many fell into the water pit below. I also saw some very smart ladies in front of me climb up on the board and work their way across with their hands and their legs crossed over the top of the board. They looked like monkeys hanging upside down from the board, except they were not holding on by their feet; they used their legs. As I watched them cross, I thought, *I can do that.* My legs have always been the strongest part of my body, and hanging upside down and crawling across the board seemed like something I could manage.

I chose the board closest to the edge so Frank could walk alongside and guide me to the end. Frank laughed at my technique as I swung my legs one over the other while working my way across the board. As I have said many times before, my upper body strength was a bit lacking then, so I didn't have the strength to reach forward with my hands and pull my body toward my hands with my legs swung over the board as most would do in this situation. Honestly, I am not even sure I thought of that as an option, either. I had a singular focus for this obstacle—to get across that dang board and not fall into the water. I didn't much care how I looked getting across it. I was going to cross it, period! So, hand over hand, leg over leg, I worked my way across the board to the other side. Success! I got across without falling into the water!

This also was the obstacle where they had the event photographer, which made for a wonderful photo op. I keep this picture of me hanging from that board on the wall in my office as a reminder that I can do anything I set my mind to do. I love that picture!

The reason I love that picture is that it captured my victory in overcoming my negative thoughts and doubts while completing that obstacle. It reminds me of the power of my mind and determination. That it doesn't matter what approach I take or how I get across, it only matters that I do. But most importantly, it reminds me not to give up on myself and that even when things look hard or the bleakest, I can persevere and get through them—if I want to. Did it matter that I didn't go across as the competitors had? No. Did it matter that I got across this thing? YES! On this obstacle, I put aside all the things that typically cause me angst and make me stop to think, *Should I even do this?* I stayed focused on the task at hand, pulling on my determination to complete it.

TAPPING INTO YOUR DETERMINATION

There were many times on that crawl across the board when I thought about giving up and letting go into the water. Like many worthy goals, there are points along the way where the process is hard, and the thought of giving up is tempting. I had nothing to prove to anyone but myself. But I wouldn't allow myself to let go or give up. I wanted to get to the other side and conquer this challenge. It frustrated me that I had walked around so many obstacles. I needed to try a hard one and succeed instead of dropping into another muddy water pit. The win was important to me, and I had something to prove to myself—I needed to prove I could do this!

Many times, overcoming obstacles is driven by your determination to get through them. It's that attitude you have that makes you stick to it no matter what. Many times in life, you need to find that determination inside you to push through life's circumstances despite it all. To meet a goal, you might have a challenge you need to overcome. People who have a sales role understand this when it comes to meeting their numbers. You inevitably get more no's than yes's but sticking to it is the only way to meet your goals. There is no other way. This is where persistence and determination intersect. If you are not determined to meet your goals, you will not choose to persist through the tough times. Tapping into your determination to continue is what sets you apart from others.

For any goal you set, there is a period where the process simply sucks! Where you feel like quitting, and you question whether the end goal is truly worth the effort. You might be training for a race, and doing another mile leaves you feeling exhausted before you even put your running shoes on. Completing a project at work makes you want to call in sick rather than sit through another meeting. Sticking to a diet or paying down debt feels like it is taking forever, and you wonder if you will ever get to where you want to be.

This is when you need to rely on your determination to stay the course. There is no other way to put it. There are times when your sheer willpower and determination are what you need to rely on to see you through to the other side. But there are things you can do to support your willpower when the road gets long, and you feel like it is taking forever to reach your goals. And you just might find some interesting byproducts of your determination.

Focus on the overall goal, not the pain

While working my way across that board, I knew I had a destination point—the other side. That was my goal. The problems that I faced while getting across were my hands slipping off the board, the board cutting into my legs, and my exhaustion at that point in the race. Each time I moved, I felt like I would slip and drop into the muddy water pit below. Getting across the board was painful and difficult. However, I knew that if I focused on the pain and difficulty, I would find a reason to give up. So instead, I focused on the end board and on each movement I made. I focused on the coaching I received from Frank and his laughing at my technique. Putting my focus there pushed my negative thoughts out of my mind.

When you face a challenge in life, switch your focus. As I mentioned in Chapter 7: Conquerors Carry, focus on the next step in the process and the accomplishments along the way. Know where your end goal is but keep your focus on the current step you are on and how to get through it. If it is running another mile, focus on the next tree or marker, not the current mile you are on or how many more you need to go. When you get there, then pick another tree or marker. Keeping your focus on these mini-goals will take your mind off the problems or pain you feel along the way.

Where you put your focus will help you find your determination. If you focus only on the problems, it will be difficult to find the determination you need to get through the challenge. Instead, focus on the little wins you make along the way. The miles you have already accomplished, a hard part of a project that is completed, debt that has been paid off, a series of days that you followed your diet, etc. Fight off the negativity by keeping a positive attitude. Knowing what is waiting for you at the end will help you keep things positive, even when things get tough.

And they will get tough. Remind yourself why you made the goal and what benefits you will receive once you reach your goal. Keeping the end in mind is one way to find your determination to persist through a challenge. Other things will help drive you as well, though.

Fear as a motivator

Another thought that kept me from letting go and dropping into the water was fear. I was pretty high up and knew if I were to let go, there was a strong possibility that I would hit the water hard on my back. That thought kept me moving forward, determined not to let go until I had made it safely to the other side.

Fear can be a powerful motivator at times. In the case of overcoming an obstacle or achieving a goal, you can use the fear of the consequences of not succeeding to positively motivate you. Each challenge presents itself with positive and negative consequences. You can use these as motivation when questioning your resolve to complete the challenge. When paying down debt, it could be what would happen if you do not get rid of the bills that you pay. How will this affect what you can afford in future years? If you are working on losing weight, what will happen if you do not shed those pounds? For a project goal at work, what consequences will you or your team face if you do not meet a deadline?

The intent is not to use fear as a negative motivator, although it can feel that way. Instead, knowing what will happen if you do not succeed can help fuel your determination when you need it to get over that hump that could easily roll you backward, halting your forward momentum.

Use Your Purpose to Drive You

Your purpose for doing something will also fuel your determination to get through it. We discussed this in Chapter 4: The Continental Divide, when I found my determination to get over that wall in my third race because I wanted to help my daughter over it. When you know why you want to do something or what purpose it serves, it helps you to persist through the challenging times.

For this obstacle, there was no one I needed to be there for to help get through the challenge, so my purpose was for me. I desperately wanted to accomplish one of these hard obstacles. I bring this up because sometimes your purpose is for you only. And that is okay. The pride you feel when you accomplish something that has been challenging to you is beneficial to your growth. It gives you pride and confidence in your accomplishments, which fuels your ability to take on bigger challenges.

So don't feel like your purpose always has to have some great meaning behind it. Those things you take on and push through for yourself are just as important as those that you take on for someone else. They can even be more important, and not in a self-centered way but in building your confidence.

Determination Fuels Confidence

When you succeed at staying the course and completing an obstacle, you increase your confidence level. It took me three races to get over the Continental Divide. So, when we came to that wall in our fourth race, I could have sworn that they shrunk the wall! Seriously! It didn't look as big and as intimidating to me as it had in previous races. And I got over it with little difficulty. What was different?

I was. I persistently took on the challenge. Once I found my purpose for getting over it, I found my determination to get over it, so I did. Now that I have conquered it, I know what to do and how difficult it is. When I come to this wall now, I no longer struggle like I did when I first took it on. I have more confidence in my ability.

This happens for any challenge you take on. To some extent, the more you succeed at something, the easier it gets to take it on again and to take on other things in life. When you overcome a challenge, your perspective changes, and your confidence increases. Each time this happens, you add fuel to your determination fire and can take on other challenges. Confidence comes from accomplishing something that was hard. Determination and persistence help push you through the challenge.

No matter what you want in life, the path is rarely easy or straightforward. You will need to test yourself, your resolve, strength, and fortitude. When you do, you will come out on the other side stronger, more resilient, and with the confidence to take on future challenges. The battles we face and persevere through strengthen us. Deciding to face and endure them makes all the difference in who we are in the end.

So with that in mind, who could you be if you stayed for the fight?

Lesson

- Your determination is fuel to take on a challenge
- What you focus on impacts your progress
- Fear and purpose can be strong motivators

Take Action

To tap into your reservoir of determination, think about the obstacles you have encountered in the past. What made you persevere even though it was challenging? What motivated you to persist through the challenge and not give up? Using the questions below, write down challenges that you have overcome through sheer determination, then analyze what got you through them and how you might use this same mental grit to overcome future obstacles.

Questions to Ponder

- What did you persist through?
- How did you do it?
- What did you focus on?
- Did something derail you? If so, what was it?
- What motivators did you use? Purpose or fear? Or both?
- What was the impact on your confidence?
- How do you perceive the same challenges today?
- What can you use to take on future challenges?

We have covered how you recover from injuries or setbacks, why discovering your purpose helps you overcome challenges, and how to use your persistence to take on the obstacles in your path. Next, we look at how we can use our creative muscles to take on the challenges that we face.

PART 4
CREATIVITY

10
WALKING THE TIGHTROPE

WHO COULD YOU INSPIRE?

*Just because something works
doesn't mean that it cannot be improved.*

– Shuri, *Black Panther*

Many obstacles in these OCRs are not tremendous physical challenges that require superior strength, but they do require you to think and strategize. They are the mental challenges that you get through by using a little creativity and curiosity instead of brute strength. The instructions (if there are any) do not tell you *how* to do them or how *not* to do them either. Most often, the instructions are minimal and more like warnings or competitor-wave guidelines or requirements, such as ". . . using your hands only" or "no feet allowed." Those of us in the non-competitor waves must figure out for ourselves how to get across each one without falling into the murky water pit below. Thankfully, many obstacles have no pit to avoid, so you only need to complete the obstacle to continue along the course.

One obstacle we encountered in our first obstacle course race in Little Rock, Arkansas, in 2015 didn't test our strength; instead, it tested our balance. This one was a set of wires strung between two nine or ten-foot boards that were set up like poles on each side of a muddy water pit. One wire was for you to walk on, and another, about waist high, was for you to hold on to as you walked on the wire below. Both wires were loose. The one you walked on was a little tighter than the one meant for you to steady yourself with, but not by much. It seemed the strategy was to walk across the wire like a tightrope walker would. But instead of falling from high heights, you fall only about two feet into the pit. It's a much safer way to learn how to walk a tightrope.

While waiting to tackle this obstacle, I noticed the waist-high wire used to balance the participant did not provide any stability at all because it was so loose. The wire caused those who depended on it to lose their balance instead of helping them, and they ended up in the water below. You could test your balancing skills and conquer this obstacle with or without the help of the wire. That was one way to take on this task and succeed. However, I didn't want to fall into the pit of water, and I really wanted to get across, so I kept thinking there had to be a way to tackle this obstacle that would accomplish both.

After watching several participants before us fall into the water, I had an idea. As Frank approached to go first, I turned to the volunteer and asked, "Can I pull the top wire taut against this pole?"

Truth be told, the volunteers do not care what you do so long as you are not doing anything stupid, which means you are not doing anything that will hurt you or someone else. The volunteer just looked at me and gave me a *"Sure, do what you like"* shrug. So before Frank started walking across the wire, I told him to hold up while I grabbed the top wire and wrapped it around the board the wires were attached to. I pulled it taut by putting my feet at the base of the pole and leaned back with the remaining wire securely in my hands, then told Frank to start his walk across the lower wire.

The lower wire was still loose, but by pulling the upper wire taut, it gave him the stability he needed to traverse over the muddy water pit without falling in. He successfully made it to the other side. Once he was back on solid ground, I let go of the wire, and Frank then returned the favor by pulling it taut for me. Proud of our success, we high-fived each other and trotted off to the next obstacle.

Looking back over my shoulder, I watched as the couple who came behind us took turns pulling the wire taut so they could walk across to the other side as we had done. Not only had we successfully gotten across, but by following our lead, those who came directly after us did as well. I am not sure how many more avoided the pit that day by using the technique we used, but I hope we started a chain reaction that helped keep others dry. At least from that obstacle!

Take a Pause and Evaluate

By taking the time to evaluate the situation, we came up with a solution. With no instructions giving us hints about what we could or couldn't do, we thought outside the box and tried something different to get across that obstacle. We could have done what others had done before us, which was to hope we had enough balance to tightrope-walk our way across, but we knew neither of us was that great of a tightrope walker, and the waist-high, loose wire didn't look very promising as a support to keep us from the water below. So instead of following what others had done before us, we came up with something new—or a slightly different strategy—and overcame that obstacle.

How many times do we do what others do without thinking there could be another way? We follow along doing the same thing because that's what others have done. Even if the results were not that good, like those who fell into the water before us. We keep repeating what others have done instead of pausing to ask ourselves if there is an easier or better option to get through the challenge, one that suits our strengths and abilities. By taking a few moments to review the challenge in front of you and evaluate your options, you might find there is an easier way for you to accomplish the task. Few things in life have to be completed exactly as others have done. Following your unique path can lead you to succeed where others have failed.

Never fear asking permission

Another obstacle we might face when challenging the status quo is asking for permission to do something. When we test boundaries or want to do something different, we might fear asking permission to try a new way. We might be concerned that we will get an answer we dislike. Someone might question why we want to do something differently, or worse, they might say no to our idea.

At that wire obstacle, the volunteer could have said no to me. He could have told me things had to stay as there were, and we weren't allowed to pull on the wire. So what if that were the answer? Was that the worst thing that could have happened at that obstacle? Not really. Falling into another pit of water would have been worse than a "no" from the volunteer, but not the end of the world!

If I had let my concerns about getting a negative answer to stop me, we would have ended up in the water pit below the wire—that I am sure of. If I hadn't asked, then I would never have known that it didn't matter if I pulled on the wire. When you come up with a creative idea or solution that you have to run by someone, don't be afraid to do so. The worst thing they could do is tell you no or dislike your idea. So what? At least you tried. At least you were thinking outside the box. You are being creative and coming up with a solution where others had not. Sure, your solution might fail, but what if it doesn't? Who else could you inspire?

Inspiring Others

This leads to another reason it is worth asking, getting creative, and trying something fresh to tackle a difficult task: others are watching. They are watching to see how you handle things and how you succeed at accomplishing the mission. Most of those watching want to see you succeed. They want to be inspired to face a challenge and feel that encouragement that they, too, could do it. Your willingness to test the norm, challenge the status quo, and succeed is inspirational and gives others hope. This is another reason we should not give up on overcoming an obstacle until we have thought through the various ways we could approach it.

Our awareness of others watching us could also stop us from trying something new (see Chapter 11 for a discussion on facing down the perfection demon). However, another way to look at it is that what we do and how we handle things could inspire others, like the ladies who went before me on the board crawl. They gave me hope that there was another way to get across that board. They inspired me to at least try it.

When you take a chance and try a different approach, no matter what others may think, you might inspire your kids, your spouse, a friend, a coworker, a colleague, or someone on Instagram whom you've never met. Frank and I will never meet the couple who followed us on that tightrope walk or those after them. But if each one watched and pulled the wire taut as we did, then each one would probably have succeeded at crossing that pit without falling in. We know, though, that we helped a few more people that day succeed at an obstacle they might not have overcome if they hadn't decided to try something different and pull on that wire.

Be willing to get creative and ask yourself if there is another way to approach a challenge other than the way others have done before you. Ask your question and face your fear of rejection. Be the example to others to inspire them to know that there is more than one way to tackle an obstacle. You only need to think about it and ask yourself, *is there another way*?

Lesson

- Pause and evaluate the challenge before you
- Don't be afraid to challenge the status quo
- Your creativity can inspire others

Take Action

Is there something that you are waiting to do because, to you, it is challenging, or maybe you cannot tackle it the way others have? Have you thought about other ways to take on this obstacle? Is there something holding you back? Take some time to explore a challenge that you feel you could accomplish but maybe not quite the same way someone else has. How would you do it differently?

Questions to Ponder

- What is the challenge?
- What is difficult for you about it?

- How have others succeeded?
- How have others failed?
- What is challenging to you?
- What could you do differently that would enable you to succeed?

Sometimes it is not only the obstacle we face that forces us to get creative but our ability to take on the challenge before us. Many times, we let perfection stand in our way of completing or even starting something. Next, we will cover some strategies to conquer the evil perfection demon.

11

WALK THE PLANK

Does perfection hold you back?

*You never know. You hope for the best,
then make do with what you get.*

—Nick Fury, *Age of Ultron*

Some OCR obstacles not only challenge your balance, but they challenge your ego as well. Under normal circumstances (although they design these courses with abnormal circumstances), you could take on the obstacle with skill and ease. However, like in life, some obstacles will test your ability to complete them perfectly. Walk the Plank was one of those obstacles for me.

In 2018, we were completing our third Conquer the Gauntlet race outside of Tulsa, Oklahoma. This time, though, we had our children with us, our son, age fifteen, and our daughter, age twelve. This was their first big obstacle course race. By then, they had completed two Warrior Dashes with us, so they were ready to take on a longer, more difficult OCR and were now old enough to do so.

Given the name of this obstacle, Walk the Plank, you might think it was over another muddy water pit. However, it wasn't. Instead, to complete this obstacle, you must walk across a set of two-inch by six-inch boards that are connected in a line about twenty feet long. The line is raised off the ground and forms peaks of varying heights. From the side, it looks like several small, uneven hills in a row.

To complete this challenge, you must walk on the six-inch board up and down these mini hills. I think the peak on the obstacle was about four feet off the ground. So it was not too high up but high enough to cause some concern if you were to lose your balance. Most people who completed this obstacle walked up and down the boards with their arms extended for balance since it's possible to complete while standing upright.

Imperfectly Done

Well, that is not exactly how I got across the boards. By the time we got to Walk the Plank, we were about two-thirds of the way through the course. When we approached this challenge, it looked easy enough, and I thought, *I can do this; not a problem!* We were alternating who went first because we had brought a camera with us to capture many of those fabulous moments we have on these courses.

This time, my family went first, which left me to bring up the rear, taking pictures. Once they finished, my daughter ran back and grabbed the camera so I could begin my trek across the planks. Oh boy! I can laugh now, but for the life of me, I could not get my balance. I stopped for a moment, thinking to myself, *this is easy; why am I having such difficulty?* Then, other thoughts quickly descended upon me: *I can't pass this up. I can't walk around this one—not when my entire family just went over it without a problem. This is silly. I've got to find a way to get over this thing!*

LESSONS FROM THE OBSTACLE COURSE

So I chose to bear-crawl across it. The pictures that my wonderful daughter took of me crawling over this thing are hilarious. Since the setup of this obstacle is several small peaks, it meant I had to turn around at the top of the peak to work my way backward down the other side. Then turn around at the bottom to work my way up to the next peak headfirst. As I bear-crawled my way across this obstacle, my daughter got a great butt shot of me crawling backward down the last peak. Yes, she thought that was quite funny.

An elegant job of completing that obstacle it was not! However, that I couldn't do it as well as my family and others had didn't stop me from accepting the challenge and completing it. Even though I knew there would be pictures later to document, for posterity, my unconventional way of getting across it, I did it anyway.

I had a few moments as I began the obstacle when I thought about not doing it because I couldn't walk across as others had. I paused briefly to wonder if it would be that bad for me to walk around it or whether I would feel embarrassed by the way I thought about tackling it. *What would my family and others think*? Those thoughts gave me pause, and when I decided to bear-crawl it, I wondered if I would regret the decision that I didn't walk "perfectly" upright across those boards.

Now I am glad I got creative and figured out how to "imperfectly" crawl across those boards that day. That I choose to tackle the obstacle and not walk around it. And I am glad my daughter found it funny enough to take a few pictures. Well, kind of glad for that last one. It does make me laugh when I see the pictures, though.

But more importantly, it reminds me not to worry about doing things "imperfectly," not to compare myself to others, not to be afraid to laugh at myself, and to go ahead and get creative about doing things that might not be "normal" or "perfect." Also, it reminds me to get out of my head and get moving on a project even if I cannot do it as well as others have, like writing this book!

Avoid Perfection Paralysis

I think many have heard this quote before from Voltaire: *"Perfection is the enemy of good"* (or greatness, or progress, depending on who else you wish to quote). If I had tried to complete this obstacle upright, I might not have made it across. Or I could have lost my balance and fallen off, maybe even hurt myself. Even though I was unable to walk across as others did, I completed it in my own "imperfect" way, which was good enough for that obstacle and for me that day.

We can say the same for many things in life. Sometimes I think we get so caught up in our worry about being different and not following the pattern or the way the experts say we should that we choose not to take on some challenges in life. We are afraid to test the status quo and to get a little creative. I saw others who did not cross the planks the way they were supposed to, so that gave me the idea that I could get across without balancing myself upright, that I could find a way, as I did, on the board crawl. A small glimpse at what is possible gets the creative juices flowing.

Crossing those planks also reminded me not to focus on what others think. Believe me; this is a constant challenge for me. If I thought too much about how silly I looked or how things were supposed to be done, I wouldn't have crossed those planks. I would have walked around it, wondering later if I could have made it across another way. How many times in life do we avoid something because we know we won't do it as well as someone else has, or we get embarrassed because we think we'll look odd or silly completing the task? We take the wind out of our sails before we have even pushed away from the dock.

Looking back on my thoughts before I crossed those planks made me realize that sometimes I am my own worst enemy. That I stop myself before I even get started because I fear what others will think because I am not doing whatever it is perfectly. For that obstacle, I had to remind myself to focus on the goal, crossing those peaks without falling off, and that nobody cared how I got across the obstacle—just that I did.

We can apply that same mental strategy to many obstacles we face in life. Does it really matter how you complete them? Is *good* good enough? If you wait to be perfect, will you ever get across? Or will you wait too long and let an opportunity pass you by? If you try to be perfect and you fail, will you be able to get back on the plank and try again? Will you try the same way, or maybe try something different that is good enough to get the job done? Must you only do it a certain way, or do you only need to complete it?

Often, when we wait for perfection, we are actually choosing not to take on something. We are making a choice not to try. When we do this, we miss out on what we could have accomplished if we had decided to push forward, perfect or not.

The comparison demon

As if worrying about what others think isn't bad enough, we harm ourselves further by comparing ourselves to them and let that stop us from facing a challenge at all. My family made it across the planks on their feet without having to bear-crawl it, so why couldn't I? Because I couldn't get across like they did, I could have let the comparison demon step in and tell me not to even try, that my way wasn't good enough, clever enough, the right way, or perfect, so why bother?

Comparing ourselves to others can be so self-defeating, yet we do it often, sometimes without even realizing it. It makes us second-guess our ability, refrain from trying new things, and robs us of our achievements.

We might also chastise ourselves, thinking we are not as good as those who succeeded at the challenge we are facing, so why should we even try? While those going before us might have more skill to accomplish the challenge, do we ever stop to ask ourselves if it is necessary to do it the way they did? What is really stopping us from completing something that is doable for us but maybe not in the same way that someone else has done it? Will we do it as perfectly as others have? Or will we do it well enough that the task is complete and that is all that is really needed?

Instead of waiting for perfection and comparing yourself to others, dare to be creative. Forge your own path. Be true to who you are. To what makes you unique.

DARE TO LAUGH

Last on this topic: don't be afraid to laugh at yourself. I know I looked silly while bear-crawling over that obstacle, and I heard my daughter laughing as I crawled. She was laughing in a good way—with me, not at me—because I was laughing too. Learn to laugh at yourself. Don't take yourself so seriously that you forget to have fun.

Laughter keeps things light, which helps keep your stress down. When you are not stressed, you are not so hard on yourself. The benefit of not being so hard on yourself means you allow yourself some grace to imperfectly get things done. Which means you find a creative way to take on the challenge. One that suits your abilities and your strengths.

Plus, studies show that laughter can actually improve your immune system, relieve pain, increase personal satisfaction, and improve your mood.[4] A side bonus to reducing stress through laughter is it just might help you live longer, which means you can take on more obstacles—imperfectly of course![5]

We tend to suck the fun out of life when we focus on perfection. Life is not supposed to be perfect. It is supposed to be lived. When you can laugh at yourself, at your follies in life, you know you are living because you are pushing yourself to get uncomfortable and to take on new things. Choose to live and laugh.

I am certain we will take on the Walk the Plank obstacle again or something similar. When we do, will I walk upright, or will I bear-crawl? I am not too sure, but I know I will get across—even if it is not perfect.

Lesson

- Imperfect but done is good enough
- Don't let the comparison demon win
- Laugh and have fun

Take Action

What have you been afraid to take on because you cannot do it perfectly? Maybe you are worried about what others will think. What would it take to get you off that fence of perfection? Using the questions below, think about a challenge you haven't taken on because you feel you are not going to do it as well as others. How can you "imperfectly" conquer it?

Questions to Ponder

- What regrets would you have if you didn't take on this obstacle?

- Is it something you can do?
- Why are you waiting?
- What are your concerns?
- What would really happen if it wasn't done perfectly or as others have done it?
- What could you learn from your experience?

For the last part of Creativity, we tackle how we can get creative despite the size of the challenge or the circumstances we find ourselves in.

12

VIRTUAL RACES

WHAT DO YOU DO WHEN THINGS DON'T GO AS PLANNED?

The world is full of evil and lies and pain and death, and you can't hide from it; you can only face it. The question is, when you do: how do you respond? Who do you become?

—Phil Coulson, *Agents of S.H.I.E.L.D.*

When we moved to Dallas, Texas, the opportunity to hit a few more races in our backyard was both exciting and convenient. Being so close, we signed up for two right away, one for the fall of 2019 and the other for the spring of 2020. However, we didn't get to do either of them as planned because of another injury and a global pandemic, both out of our control.

Knowing more about this obstacle course world we had embarked upon, we wanted to try two popular race themes next, the Tough Mudder race and a Spartan race. Still learning the difference and opportunities these races provided, we figured we would start with the two that were in our new backyard, then try a few others in their respective series. The

Tough Mudder we signed up for would be in September 2019, and the Spartan race, in their stadium series, was to be in June 2020.

One challenging thing about signing up for any race is that many things could prevent you from attending. I have signed up for several running races I could not attend because of an activity commitment our kids had, such as a football practice or lacrosse tournament. And as much as we reviewed schedules before we signed up, it was always possible for our event to get bumped because of another family or work obligation.

When we signed up for the Tough Mudder, we had a few things we thought might bump the race, like football practice and the move-in date for our house. But we hoped for the best and signed up anyway.

As race day approached, we were grateful that it looked like nothing was going to derail our September date. That was until Frank broke his hand during the move into our house. Well, it was his pinky finger at the base of his hand, but still, it was broken, and his hand was swollen and taped. It seems ridiculous as I type this to say we decided not to do the race because of a broken pinky finger, but do you know how much you use your pinky in these races? Honestly, there were several reasons why we decided to postpone this race, but the broken pinky was the final nail in the coffin.

Frank is our base. He is our family Rock in these races (a topic I will discuss further in Chapter 14). Not having him at his full capacity for the race would have put a major damper on the day. We know this because we have been through it before. Had this been our first obstacle course race, we might have considered going and probably would have. Frank would have endured it as he had done in previous races and would have put on his best face. However, since that would have been our first Tough Mudder race, we all wanted to enjoy the fun of the race and having Frank's hand wrapped and not completely usable would have made the day miserable for all of us. Plus, we had a full house to unpack. Frank was already doing his best to move boxes with a wrapped hand, but that was a challenge all on its own. Hence, an obstacle course would not have been much fun that day. So we punted and requested to move the race to another date in 2020—yeah, *that* 2020.

Control what you can

When the clock rolled over to January 1, 2020, I think most of us were excited about what the new decade had in store for us. None of us could have expected a global pandemic would shut the world down. So before we knew what 2020 would bring, we had narrowed in on a date for the punted Tough Mudder and had signed up for the Spartan stadium race at AT&T Stadium in Dallas, Texas. We had unpacked, settled in, and healed—again.

Then March came, and all plans changed. This time it wasn't our choice to punt or postpone a race because of an injury or a family obligation. Like everyone, we had to forfeit it, and we couldn't even make a secondary plan right away to try again in a few months. With the rest of the world, we had to wait, and wait, and wait some more.

Saying that 2020 didn't go as planned for any of us is probably the understatement of the century. How many of us had plans that had to be changed, adjusted, postponed, or canceled completely? All of us. So we couldn't be upset that they canceled our first Spartan race. That was minor compared to all the other things that happened in 2020. However, we were still a little disappointed; like many fellow obstacle course participants, this was a 2020 event we were looking forward to.

Every one of us had something we were looking forward to in 2020. Big or small, not being able to do something you had planned because of something out of your control is a disappointment, no matter how you look at it. How you handle your disappointment will have a big impact on how you manage it, which will determine how creative you can get in overcoming it.

I know that missing an obstacle course event is *very* minor compared to all that went on in 2020. I cannot stress that enough. It is a blip on the screen of all that transpired that year. So handling our disappointment is nothing compared to the big events that were postponed or canceled or the major tragedies that occurred in 2020.

With this in mind, we will discuss how we got creative and handled the canceled events we looked forward to in the midst of uncertainty. This is about how you control what you can and how your reactions impact your decision-making skills.

Staying the course to be creative

The main part of our strategy was to stick with the workout routine we had so that we could keep moving forward physically. Doing so helped us stay in shape, which meant we would be ready for whenever we could participate in our next obstacle course race. A side benefit was that it allowed us to burn off nervous energy caused by all the uncertainty. The thing about keeping with our routine is that it kept life as normal as possible for us during this period. It was something we could control amidst all the things we couldn't.

The other benefit to keeping to a routine of exercise was that it helped burn off some stress. Any time you can reduce your stress, you enable yourself to process things better and think more clearly. When you can think clearer, you can allow your creative juices to flow. So finding an outlet that you enjoy or that gets you to focus on something within your realm of control, allows you to find your calm, and will clear your mind of distractions, especially the negative ones. Which means your decision-making process is stronger, and the endorphins that are released help you feel better. It's a win / win!

In 2020, many people faced several canceled events that would have otherwise helped them stick with their routines. Obstacle course curators were no different. Since we couldn't do any races in person for most of 2020, many event sponsors had to get creative. Their creativity led to the birth of virtual races. At first, it was odd, but like millions of people around the globe, we jumped at the opportunity to do something that would take us beyond the four walls of our homes. Even though we couldn't be part of a live event, we signed up to do a few Spartan and Tough Mudder virtual races throughout the remainder of 2020.

The structure of these virtual races was to run the distance of the race and do a set of "obstacles," which were body-weight moves you could do with no equipment, such as squats, lunges, push-ups, sit-ups, etc. You were to record your run on an app that could capture your run data and log your information onto their websites to signify that you completed the virtual race. You could even post some pictures on social media for good measure or as proof that you actually did the exercise obstacles.

For the Spartan races, you had anywhere from fifteen to thirty different bodyweight exercises to do, along with either a 5 km, 10 km, or half-marathon run. The Tough Mudder was different and harder to explain. We actually got confused about the whole thing and didn't complete as much as we thought we would. Or maybe we did; I am still not sure. Either way, we tasked ourselves with completing these challenges during the summer of 2020. How we did them was where we got creative.

Do Things Your Way

While participating in a live event, you usually run a mile or so, then do an obstacle. This pattern continues throughout the length of the course, alternating between running and obstacles. The virtual race instructions seemed to imply you should run all the miles and then do all the "obstacles" or vice versa. Well, for several reasons, I didn't want to do it that way.

Even though I have completed several long runs in the past, such as 10 km events and half-marathons, I was not looking forward to doing all the running and then the "obstacles" the virtual events required. So I broke them down as we would experience them in an actual event. This is where the creativity part comes in. If we had twenty "obstacles" to do and a three-mile run, I would break down the obstacles into four sets of five and run a mile in between each set of obstacles. It made the event feel more like a true obstacle course challenge versus a run with exercises after it. We broke down each one like this, never doing more than about three miles in between the required obstacles. My husband was more inclined to get the run out of the way and then do the obstacles, but he humored me and went along with my little plan. We had fun and got through about four different races in 2020.

Similar to our discussion in the previous chapters, part of being creative is finding your own way to take on the obstacles before you. The difference here is taking a loose set of guidelines and making the process yours despite what might be going on around you. It is hitting that pause button, focusing on what you can control, and deciding what you want the outcome to look like. Doing this in stressful, or not so stressful, situations helps you control the outcome as best you can. When you have more control over the process, you will enjoy it more, and you will be able to manage through the chaos around you better.

Manage Your Mind

In life, we handle disappointments all the time, some big and some small. Whatever the size of the event, it is how we handle our disappointment that sets the tone for how creative we can get to overcome these setbacks. We have had larger disappointments than not being able to participate in a couple of obstacle races, such as infertility, brain surgery, job losses, serious illnesses of family members, losing a very dear friend way too early in her life, and many others. However, life does go on, and we must find a way to live life to the best of our abilities, no matter how hard at times it may seem to do so.

Sometimes, to get through life's disappointments, we need to get a little creative. When we had fertility issues, we had to adjust to several things in our lives, from treatment options to the possibility we couldn't have children. Now you have heard me mention our kids frequently, so you know how that turned out. But it wasn't without facing several disappointments throughout the process. Because of each disappointment, we focused on overcoming the pregnancy obstacle as best we could.

Throughout that process, we had to get a little creative in how we handled some things we had to do. Each time, we faced the obstacle with humor and almost took it as a challenge to see how creative we could get. Especially when certain things, such as sperm mobility, had to be tested. This made the process and repeated monthly disappointments more bearable.

Having an accurate perspective on the situation also allows your creative juices to get flowing. How big is the disappointment that you are facing? Is there a solution that you could come up with that would help you make the most of the situation? If the issues are not all that bad, like switching from in-person to virtual races, what can you do to still enjoy the day or event? How do you make lemonade out of the lemons you have?

Life might not go the way you had intended or thought it should, but that is life. Sometimes big things will set you back. But sometimes, it's the smaller things that trip us up more. I find it interesting that sometimes I feel more equipped to handle the big obstacles I face in life than the small ones. It could be that I have a different mindset when big issues take over our lives. When something big happens, I know I need to come up with a way to manage through the situation, like we did when Frank had brain surgery. Many things could have gone wrong, and the outcome could have been much worse. For me, when the big things happen, I find I am better at accepting the situation and dealing with what I have been given. When small things come up, though, I have a much different reaction—at first.

Managing the Small Things

It's the little triggers in life that can change the day and the way we handle the obstacles we face. When small things or events occur, it can be easy to lose our coping mechanisms. This could happen for many reasons. It could be you are stressed about something else going on. Or you have had a hectic week and have a lot on your plate. Maybe you are hungry and just need to refuel. Whatever the underlying circumstances are, when something small or minor comes up, you might not handle the obstacle before you as well as you are able to. When we do not handle things as well as we should, it is harder to get creative and manage through the obstacle before us.

So the first thing we need to control is how we react when things don't go our way. In Chapter 2, we discussed how you first react to disappointment. When something doesn't go the way you had intended, how you handle your immediate reaction to a problem will set the tone for how well you can manage the challenge before you. Once we have our emotions in check, now what? What can you do to still make the most out of the situation?

Let's say you are on a family vacation, and they cancel an excursion you had scheduled because of some unforeseen event. Do you sit around the hotel and mope? Or do you find something else to do that day and fill your time? Could you do another activity that you had wanted to do but didn't have the time for before the cancellation? Or maybe you could use another day to relax, play board games, or enjoy your family or whomever you are traveling with.

The same is true for so many other things that can derail you in life and business. Pay attention to your immediate reactions when things don't go as you thought they would. Be mindful of what you say and how you react. Learning what triggers you to go careening off the deep end will help you take back control of the situation before you. Which means you will be better equipped to take on the obstacle and succeed. So now that you have your reactions under control, what do you do when others don't?

Managing other's reactions

It also helps to recognize not only how you react to change but also how others will react. How do you get everyone back on board and working toward a solution rather than being stuck in the disappointment?

I know now that our son does not like change. It took me a while to recognize this, so when our plans changed, it threw him into a tizzy. We argued, he got into trouble for talking back, and things didn't go so well. Once I figured out that it was the change in direction that had him careening off the tracks, I learned how to prepare him better for our changing plans. As he has matured, we found we could discuss with him the change in direction, and he could handle it better because he was now more aware that he doesn't like it when plans change. We still have problems when plans change every once in a while, but we are all getting better at communicating with each other when we must make slight adjustments to our plans.

Same can be said when plans change at work or with friends. Communication, understanding, and perspective are key attributes when dealing with how others face challenges. We all like to handle our obstacles our own way. When something happens, we also react to change differently. If you are in a leadership position, you need to be able to take a step back and evaluate the situation at hand and how others are reacting to it. Know they most likely will not react the same way you do to the same situation, and you cannot expect them to. Be sure to openly communicate about whatever it is the organization is facing, what obstacles need to be overcome, and the plan to do so.

Understand there will be pushback, hesitation, and uncertainty, as well as all the emotions that come with these reactions. Take the time to address those feelings and provide assurance that the direction that has been chosen was done so with care and consideration for all those involved. Doing so will not only help you get on back on track faster but will also reduce the emotional stress that comes along with change.

Pause before action

What happens when a project at work gets derailed? How do you get it back on track? Do you need to pivot and try something else? How quickly can you evaluate the situation and look for ways to still get the job done? Sometimes the obstacle is there because that is not the way you are supposed to complete the task at hand. If you stopped to evaluate, you might find you were heading down the wrong path anyway. When you stop to look at things differently, you find a better way to accomplish the task, like we had covered in Chapter 10 when we pulled on the upper wire to allow for more stability as we crossed the lower wire.

It's that pause before action that allows you time to collect yourself, process the situation, then come up with a solution, giving you a clearer head to take on the challenge before you.

Keep proper perspective

Maybe it is the military wife in me, but I do try very hard to keep proper perspective on the challenges we face. Most of the challenges we will face in our lives are not life-and-death situations. Instead, they are a part of life and come up more frequently than the larger challenges or situations we may face. As I mentioned earlier, coming up with options for the races we missed was minor in comparison to all that transpired in 2020. But that is the point—it was minor. So we could let our disappointment derail us, or we could keep things in perspective, understanding that this is only a hiccup in our plans, and we could find a way to participate. And still have fun.

How you handle the minor things in life and having the ability to think of replacement activities or a different way to handle those obstacles can affect so many other things in your life, such as your stress level! Take the little things in stride while still meeting the challenge with grace and a little creativity. Doing so, you will set yourself up for great things in your future.

And as a side note: when events opened up again in 2021, we finally got to complete two Spartans and a Tough Mudder event. It was a long journey to get to these events, but we were happy to have at last earned those medals and headbands! And are looking forward to earning many more. This is a reminder to not let go of your dreams, even if it takes a few more years to realize them. Stay the course no matter what life throws at you!

Lesson

- Have a routine or make one
- Manage your reactions
- Keep perspective

Take Action

Look back to what you wrote in Chapter 2 about an event that derailed your plans. Now take this a step further. Looking at the event, how could you take on the challenge once you have managed your immediate reaction? What could you do to still accomplish the mission or conquer the obstacle? With this challenge in mind, review the questions below to see if you can come up with a creative way to now overcome this obstacle.

Questions to Ponder

- What perspective do you now have?
- Is this a mountain or a hill?

- What options come to mind?
- What outcome do you seek?
- Is this still possible?
- What challenges do you see?
- What resources do you have to manage the challenges you see?

Getting creative can be challenging, but when you do, there are so many things you can take on that you didn't think you could before. Lean into your curiosity and adventure. You never know where it might take you.

The final strategy we will discuss is how you collaborate with others to take on the many challenges we all face in this life.

PART 5
Collaboration

13

BOARDWALK

WHO ARE YOU WALKING WITH?

We are Groot!

—Groot, *Guardians of the Galaxy*

One cool thing to come out of our obstacle course journey is that our kids now participate in these races with us. That means that not only do we get to spend time with them on the courses, but we have watched them grow with us as we take on more race challenges. We have seen them grow in their confidence and have watched them come to appreciate that there are things you simply cannot take on by yourself. Knowing how to work together to overcome an obstacle has helped them with their team sports and highlighted for all of us how important teamwork and collaboration are in all facets of our lives.

As we move on to Collaboration, we have now moved into the team aspect of completing obstacles, not only in races but also in life. You need balance and a lot of teamwork to take on many of the obstacles in these courses. I mentioned one earlier in Chapter 10 when we discussed how Frank and

I worked together to navigate the tightrope walk. However, that obstacle could have been done on your own if you were willing to take it on and had great balance. For these next few chapters, we will discuss the obstacles on these courses that are not only easier to take on as a team, but some require you to team up in order to be able to complete them.

A Little Balance Goes a Long Way

The Boardwalk is similar to the wire obstacle in that you could take this one by yourself if you have good balance. However, I seem to struggle in this area, so I find it much easier to walk across with someone else. This obstacle has participants walk twenty-one feet across a board that is only about four inches wide and hangs over a muddy water pit without anything for you to hold on to for balance.

 These boards were a little more challenging because not only was it a narrow walk, like a balance beam, but it also was a long walk. The board did not have any supports across this 21-foot span, so as you walked across, it wobbled a little. Which means *you* wobble a lot and must steady yourself as you walk across. That is difficult if you have challenges balancing yourself or you have nothing to steady yourself with.

 In this obstacle, they position many boards over the pit about four feet apart. As we watched, awaiting our turn, we saw a few people get across on their own, but we saw many more fall into the murky pit below, which, for this race, was extra muddy!

 When it was time for our 12-year-old daughter and me to walk across, we decided we could do this one better together, not separate. The space between the boards was close enough for us to reach out and hold hands as we walked across. We wobbled a little, but not enough to drop us into the mud below. We crossed that obstacle by using each other for balance. Satisfied that we had conquered another obstacle, we moved on to the next one.

For that obstacle, we needed a little help with our balance. We watched as some others got across by themselves, but not without considerable effort, like our fifteen-year-old son. He made it across on his own, but I must admit, watching him was entertaining. He bent backward and forward while he walked sideways on the board as he tried to balance himself while the board wobbled beneath him. He made it across without falling. However, we got across faster and without all the extra effort because we worked together. We did little more than hold each other's hands. That was enough to steady ourselves, so it took little effort to walk across the board.

In life, you often need a helping hand to get through the obstacle before you. You might be capable of handling the obstacle on your own, but in doing so, it will take a considerable amount of effort, as with my son crossing the board. We could have crossed that board by ourselves, but why do so when holding on to each other's hands gave us the balance we needed to get across with little effort?

Plus, it was fun. As we wobbled, my daughter and I laughed while we worked to balance each other so we could finish walking across. It was much more fun to partner with her on this obstacle than to do it alone. There are many obstacles in life that are the same. If you partnered with a coworker to complete a work project, you might get it done much sooner and with less stress.

How about parenting? I can speak for the ladies here in saying sometimes we take on too much for the family and in parenting our children. If we asked our partner to help with some tasks, we might have a little less stress—hint, hint!

Getting help makes things easier

When you work with someone else on a task, not only will you get through the obstacle, but you also gain your helper's perspective and learn how to balance each other. You learn what it takes to walk that board together, each of you taking turns to be the support for the other through the obstacle. You learn what the other person needs and how to communicate to them what you need.

By balancing each other, you increase your chances of completing the task. As we watched many people go solo over those boards, about half ended up in the pit. We didn't stick around to see how many succeeded by working together, but I think I could say more than 50 percent made it over those boards by working with someone else.

It's hard to admit that you need help with something, but it might also be the smartest thing that you could do. Setting your ego aside to allow others to help can be a challenge. My son was determined to get across this beam on his own and did not want to work with anyone to get across. That was fine, but he made it more difficult on himself by doing so. However, he has the satisfaction of completing this obstacle by himself. Sometimes that is what we are looking for and need. The only downside to that strategy was that Frank had to manage on his own since he was the last one to complete the obstacle. He got across as well, with some of the same challenges that our son had.

Asking for help does not mean that you cannot do the obstacle by yourself. But if you partnered with someone on an obstacle or task in life, would that make it easier on you and your partner? Could you get through it faster and with more ease? Could working together provide some insight into your abilities and theirs?

Lessons from the Obstacle Course

Better Outcomes

I think sometimes we are too stubborn and feel we must do things on our own. I noticed that about myself and my husband. For Frank, it could be the Marine coming out, but sometimes it seems he takes the hard way when there is an easier way to do things.

Once, I asked Frank about not asking for help on some projects.

"It's a challenge that I must take on," was his reply.

Must you really? was my thought. Maybe, but what if it isn't necessary?

For some obstacles, you have nothing to prove and lots to gain by working with someone, which is overlooked sometimes because of ego, oversight, or a feeling that you shouldn't ask for help. I challenge that thought. Not that you should or should not get help on certain things, but what will the outcome be if you get a little assistance or work with someone else to get through an obstacle or task? How would that change your process, the time to get through it, or the burden on yourself and someone else? How would it change the outcome?

Parenting is a great example of that. It never fails that one parent usually thinks they must take on more than the other. Sometimes that is true, but it also could be a lack of communication between the parents. Working together to solve parenting issues always turns out better than working at it alone. Balancing each other, as my daughter and I did on those beams, is a magical thing when raising kids. When Frank and I are united and are working together on any family project or issue, the outcome is usually so much better. There is less confusion and arguing because we balance each other in our decision-making and our efforts.

Business can be the same way. Yes, you can take on tasks by yourself, and just like many obstacles on the course, you must. But many tasks go so much smoother, quicker, and better when working with a partner. Working with another person can even be enjoyable and make the task less burdensome for both of you. The other person might have strengths you do not, and vice versa. Recognizing when a little help is needed or when partnering with someone on a project is in everyone's best interest and will help you move through business obstacles much faster and with less effort than if you were to do them on your own.

Ask yourself, what is the outcome you are seeking and what help would get you there faster? Who has the skills to take on this challenge in your organization, and how would that benefit the project? By getting a little help, will this project get done faster and with more ease? These are just a few questions you can ask yourself to see if all you need is a little balance in completing the challenge before you.

And you never know—you might even find the task more enjoyable with someone else along for the ride.

Lesson

- Identify when it is beneficial to work with someone else
- Understand what type of help is needed
- Don't let your ego stand in your way from getting a little help

Take Action

Where in your business or your personal life could you use a little balancing help? What things do you take on that, maybe if you got a little help, would make your life less stressful, make things easier? When you think about getting help, be careful not to get trapped in the "woe is me—if I only had a little help" attitude. That is not what this is about, nor will it help you much. This is really about looking at where you can improve and what strides you could make if you decided to work and communicate with another person to get a task completed or get through an obstacle. It is about building collaboration with another person, so you are both better off when you work together than when you work alone.

Questions to Ponder

- When did working with another person go well? What could you repeat?
- When did it fall apart? What happened?
- What does collaboration with another person mean to you?
- What could you achieve if you worked with someone else?
- Do you have a difficult time asking for help?
- If so, why? What would happen if you did?
- What struggles do you have that could be less challenging if you worked with someone else?
- What could that free you up to do?
- What resources do you have to manage the challenges you see?

Working with someone is one way to take on an obstacle, but some challenges require more than a little balancing from another person—they require a rock-solid foundation. Next, we will discuss that person in your life who is always there and what important role they play.

14

WALLS OF FURY

WHO'S YOUR ROCK?

You've got me? Who's got you?

—Lois Lane, *Superman*

Do you recall those first walls of the Conquer the Gauntlet race I mentioned in Chapter 1? The ones we saw as we walked from the parking lot to the starting gate? They were five, eight-and-a-half-foot walls set up in a row like dominos, with no more than about ten feet between them. As we walked from the parking lot, we watched with curiosity as people struggled to get over them. While we watched, we saw several people walk around while others ran, jumped, and grabbed the top, rolled over, then did the same thing again on the wall only ten feet away. My thought, and if I am being honest here, my worry when I saw this was, *how in the world am I going to get over these things?* After a glance at my husband, I followed that thought with a calm one. *I'll deal with those when I get to them. No need to worry about them now.* This is another good lesson or life strategy but not the focus of this chapter.

This next part of the Collaboration strategy is about identifying your *Rock*, and I do not mean Dwayne Johnson. Although I wouldn't mind that! No, I am talking about the person who is always there for you in good times and bad. The one you know you can always count on to be the support you need when life gets challenging or you think you cannot accomplish something on your own. That is the Rock we will discuss now. We will take on why it is so important to have this person in your life and why you need to be that person for others.

Why your Rock is important

The first time we encountered these walls was in our first obstacle course race in Little Rock, Arkansas, in 2015. They placed those walls toward the end of the race, which, in my humble opinion, is an awful place to put them. Although, I imagine there is a diabolical reason for doing such a thing! After completing about three-and-a-half miles of terrain and twenty obstacles before this obstacle, if we were not already tired enough, these walls would surely exhaust us. This was the race where Frank had hurt his arm, but that didn't stop him from trying to tackle the walls, and I'm pretty certain that only made his injured arm worse.

I knew I would have difficulty with these walls. I am about five-foot-six-inches, with no vertical to speak of. So jumping up to grab the top of a wall was not going to happen. That fact, along with my struggle and failure with the first seven-foot wall to get into the starting pen, made the outlook of completing this obstacle on my own not very promising. I gave these walls a sideways glance, wishing I was strong enough to run, jump, and grab the top to pull myself over as I saw others do. Instead, with a wave of my hand, I began to walk around them. As I turned away from the walls, Frank asked if I wanted to get over them. I looked at him with a puzzled stare, wondering how we could make that work. Not getting over the Rockies, those angled walls we encountered earlier in the course, still bugged me. And they weren't nearly as intimidating as these walls were, so to redeem myself, I wanted to at least make an effort to tackle these.

As I mentioned before, these five walls were set in a row about ten feet apart. Four angled boards held up each side of the wall, like many other obstacles we had encountered on the course that day. The top of the angle was probably at five feet, maybe a little lower. The angled boards provided a sturdy support for the walls, but they were too awkward to use as leverage to work your way up and over the wall. Believe me, I tried using them, but even my long legs didn't help me there.

We also tried the foot-in-the-handhold technique that we had used on so many walls before this one, but the wall was too tall for me to get high enough to grab the top and pull myself over. Not to mention, I didn't have the upper body strength to reach with my hands and pull myself up to the top of the wall from the height that the handhold gave me. So after some consideration, Frank offered to be my ladder, which meant being my Rock.

What transpired next got us a few laughs and curious stares, but it worked and is now how we take on these walls whenever we encounter them in races. Frank put his back to the wall so he could do a wall squat which gave me a place to put my foot. First, I placed my foot on the top part of his thigh, close to his stomach. Next, I hopped a little from my foot on the ground with my hands on his shoulders to get myself to the same level as my foot on his thigh. From there, holding on to the wall for balance, I placed my next foot on his shoulder. Good thing he has broad shoulders—and not only in the literal sense! Another little hop off my foot on his leg, and now I was standing on his shoulders.

From there, I could reach the top of the wall with enough height to pull myself further up while he stood up, giving me even more height and more leverage. Once I had myself situated to roll over the top of the wall, Frank ran to the other side of the wall and guided my feet as I dropped to the ground. After repeating this pattern on another wall, I no longer needed his help to get down. I was now confident enough in the distance I needed to drop and my ability to lower myself down the other side of the wall that I could do that part on my own.

Without Frank's help, I couldn't have made it over those walls, and in future races with our kids, he did the same thing for both our daughter and me. We have this strategy down now, after encountering similar walls in this race and others, that we can now complete these obstacles quickly and with little issue.

Frank has not only been my Rock in these races but also in many other things in our life. From getting promotions to losing jobs, moving across the country, fertility issues, raising kids, and so many other obstacles we have encountered in our lives, he is always there, and I am always there for him and for the family as well. We take turns being that rock-solid person who the family needs because even Rocks need a break every once in a while.

The many roles of a Rock

This strategy goes beyond your family too. I have friends that come to me, and I go to them when life gets challenging, when I need someone to listen to me, support me, or both. Having that friend who you know will always be there for you is such a blessing in life. I would love to say we are all superhuman, able to take the world on our shoulders without shrugging, but we both know that is not possible. We all need someone who we can rely on. Who we know will be there for that 3 a.m. call when we have been crying all night and need someone to talk to—the friend who will sit or walk with you as you work out a problem.

Having a Rock in your life makes things so much easier to deal with. This goes for business as well. Who do you count on at work? Who at work is that go-to person who you know will always be there, not only to get the job done but maybe as a mentor or as a guide? Do you have someone you can communicate with and strategize with? Who is there to bounce ideas off of or help with a project, or the person you know who will always be a good sounding board for you?

Don't forget, though; it goes both ways. Sometimes you need to be the Rock, the one people can come to for help or guidance, to listen to their problem, or jump in when they see a need on the team. It's not only important to have a Rock you can lean on but to take turns being one as well.

Open communication with your Rock

Communication with your Rock is important too. To get over that wall, Frank and I had to communicate with each other. We needed to discuss what each of us must do to get me over those walls, to try a few things, and not get irritated with each other when something didn't work well. We kept trying different things and talking about how we thought we could get me over the top. I also had to be very clear in my communication with him. Even though he was my ladder, I needed to tell him how I planned to get over these walls with him as my foundation. And I had to accept his advice as we strategized the climb. We kept an open dialogue so we could understand where each of us was in the process.

He also had to know when it was time to let me do some things on my own, like dropping from the other side without his help. He ran around the first two walls to guide my feet and let me know how much further I had to go. Once I got a feel for the space I had to clear in my drop, I was more comfortable dropping to the ground on my own. He still guided me a little by telling me how much further I had to go, but I didn't need his physical assistance anymore.

When we helped our daughter over, it was the two of us. Frank was on the side for her to climb, and I was on the other side to guide her down. After the first wall, she was pretty much done with my assistance, which she made crystal clear. We were still working on tactful communication then! However, she still used her father as a ladder to climb up the wall, which meant they had to have an open dialogue about how she wanted to accomplish that climb and how her father was going to help her. Each had to accept suggestions from the other.

As a Rock, it is important to know when the other person no longer needs your assistance. Understanding when someone can take on the task by themselves also requires an open dialogue between the two of you, so you know when to move from a mentor or Rock position to that of a guide to then let them fly on their own. This takes insight and truly hearing what the other person is saying. That is a task easier said than done, especially with parenting, but one we all need to practice.

In life, we will have several people who will fill the role of our Rock and several who we will be that Rock for. Sometimes, we are acknowledged for the help we give, but most times, we are not. Most Rocks are there because they know they are needed, and they have a desire to help. To make a difference in someone's life, to help see someone succeed, or to be there when times are tough. This role is a foundation role in our lives and our societies; without it, we could not accomplish all the amazing things that we do.

Lesson

- Identify who the Rock is in your life
- Understand why it is important to maintain open communication
- Know when it is time to let go

Take Action

So, who is your Rock? Who is that person who helps you through the hard times? Who is there when things get tough? Who is that person that helps steady you when you feel you are about to fall over? Why is this person so important in your life, and what have you been able to accomplish because they are always there for you?

And most importantly, have you thanked them lately?

Questions to Ponder

- Who is your Rock?
- What have you been able to accomplish with their help or support?
- Why is this so important to you?
- What would have happened if they were not there?
- Who are you a Rock for?
- How has this helped you overcome your challenges?
- What does it mean to you to be the Rock for someone else?

There is one more part of Collaboration that is so unique to these races, a trait I wish that more in our society would use to respond to the challenges we all face. It is the all-hands-on-deck approach to getting through the obstacles on the course.

15

TIGER TRAP, GREAT WALL OF AMERICA, AND MORE

WHO'S YOUR TEAM?

You think you're the only superhero in the world? Mr. Stark, you've become part of a bigger universe. You just don't know it yet.

—Nick Fury, *Iron Man*

When have you felt as if you were part of a team and something bigger than you? When have you felt as if everyone was your friend and wanted to help you succeed at whatever it was you were doing? This feeling of kindred spirits is one of the neatest things about participating in these obstacle course races. There are many obstacles on these courses where you need others' help to make it through. Where from my viewpoint, they are virtually impossible to do on your own. Could you? Maybe, but it would be extremely difficult to do so. However, if you had a helping hand, or two, or many, you could get through the challenge and mark it complete!

In these races, you find that you not only need a little help, but you also need to help others to get through some of the course obstacles. What is so neat about participating in these challenges is that a group of complete strangers will turn around and lend a helping hand to others without pause.

There are several obstacles like this in the many OCRs out there, but for this chapter, we will focus on three that we encountered on the Conquer the Gauntlet course: the Great Wall of America, the Tiger Trap, and the Belly of the Beast.

When to Jump in and Help Others

The Great Wall of America obstacle is a wall that's twelve-and-a-half-foot high and about thirty-two feet wide. On each side are wood slats about two inches deep at about the four-foot and eight-foot intervals. The objective is to get yourself to that two-inch piece of wood four feet off the ground, then from that narrow ledge, proceed to the next slat four feet above the one you are standing on. From that eight-foot-high two-inch ledge, you then needed to get yourself over the top and climb down the other side using similar two-inch-deep slats placed at the eight-foot and the four-foot-high levels.

As we approached this wall with the kids, we stopped to watch the group in front of us maneuver their way over the wall. It was a group of two men and one woman. The guys got over and then waited at the top to help their lady friend get over the top. When you are standing on that two-inch ledge that is four feet down the other side of the wall, your reach down the side you just climbed up is not that far unless you have really long arms! The woman tried twice to use the ledge and the angle piece that was holding up the wall to work her way up the wall. However, she was a little too short to get a good foothold on either the ledge or the angled piece holding up the wall. This meant she was having difficulty getting herself onto that first two-inch ledge so she could reach the hands that were outstretched above her to help pull her to the next ledge, then over.

Without really thinking about it, I jumped in to help. I walked over to her and said, "I can give you a boost if you like." She looked at me with a bit of a bewildered expression, so I felt I needed to explain further. "Put your foot in my hands. I will give you a boost up." As I said this, I clasped my hands together, palm side up, so she could see this was a place for her to place her foot. She finally got what I was saying and, with some hesitancy, put her foot in my clasped hands and reached up to the top of the angled bracket to help pull herself up. I braced myself against the wall, crouched down so she could reach my hands, and then as she steadied herself on the wall, I stood up with her foot firmly leveraged in my hands. This gave her the height she needed to reach up further and make her way to the next ledge with the help of her friends at the top. Together, as a team, we got her over.

With a quick wave to each other, their little band moved on, leaving Frank and me to help the kids get over. We did the same thing with the kids. Frank went over first so he could position himself at the top to help pull each of us up and over. We got the kids over by me using my hands as their first point of leverage like I did for the woman before us, and Frank being at the top point to help steady and pull them over.

Now that my family was over, it was my turn to get myself over, which left me at the bottom of this wall in the same predicament the woman was before us. As I made a few feeble attempts to use the angled piece to help leverage and pull myself over, a very kind man came up behind me and asked if he could help. Relieved, I accepted. He clasped his hands together, palm side up, forming a foothold for me like I had done for my family and the woman before us. He stood up as I stood up so I could reach further up the wall to my husband's outstretched hands. Without his help, I most likely would not have made it over that wall. But with his help, I did.

Helping hands

I couldn't tell you what he looks like and could never point him out in a crowd, but I am forever thankful that he had the giving spirit to lend a hand—or two. Just like the man did on the top of the Continental Divide who helped me get my daughter over the top of that beast. He didn't have to stop to help; he could have easily moved on. But that is not the point of these races. The point is to turn and help one another where you can whenever you see someone struggling, whether it be a stranger or your team, preferably both. Being there to help each other is an important part of these races, as it should be in life.

The many roles we play

The Tiger Trap is another doozy of an obstacle. It is a pit with steep walls of slippery, muddy dirt that you are to slide into, then claw your way out the other side. Sometimes the pit has water in the bottom, sometimes not. I was grateful we didn't have water in the pit we slid into in that 2018 Tulsa, Oklahoma, race with our kids. It was only thick, sticky mud.

This was the second obstacle we encountered with our kids on the course that day, so everyone still had amped-up adrenalin, and we were not that dirty—yet. Our son was raring to go, so he opted to slide in first, then I went, followed by our daughter, then my husband. Again, our Rock stayed in the pit as we worked to get the kids out of it. To get out of this pit, you must have teamwork. It is extremely helpful, if not imperative, that at least one person is at the top of the pit to pull you out and one at the bottom as leverage or to give you a good shove. I haven't seen anyone get out on their own, although I am sure there have been a few to do so.

To get out of the pit, we relied on those who got out before us, then those who slid into the pit after us. That is the purpose of this pit; it encourages true teamwork with complete strangers. We helped a fellow racer get enough leverage to reach the outstretched hands above him by placing our hands against the wall, forming a ledge for him to put his foot on. Using our hands as leverage, he could get enough height to reach the outstretched hands above him by the people who lay in the mud so they could reach into the pit and pull him out. Then it was our turn. Our son went first.

Initially, there was one guy to help our son; then another laid down to help pull him out of the pit. Once our son was up, he took the place of one of the guys at the top. That left him and the same guy who we helped get out of the pit moments before to get me out of the pit.

Now that I was out, he turned and went on his way, leaving our son and me to get our daughter and Frank out of the pit. Our daughter was easy to get out. At twelve years old, she had long legs and arms and was light. As for the big guy? Well, that is an entirely different experience! It took me, our son, and a guy who had jumped into the pit behind us to get Frank out. Once Frank was out, he and our son pulled up the guy who had helped push Frank out. We helped him get one more person out then we went on our way.

Teamwork makes the dream work! I am sure you have heard that before. Often, it is true. Getting out of the pit was a great example of how working as a team methodically can make a daunting, difficult task doable. Whether with your family, friends, or co-workers, working together is the only way you can get things done.

Could you get out of the pit by yourself? Maybe, probably, eventually, but boy, that would be difficult! Not only is it better to get help on a difficult task, but it can also be so much more fun, not to mention faster and easier. Some things in life and in business require a team effort. Learning how to be a member of the team and doing your part will move you forward in life much faster than if you were to do so by yourself.

Also, learn when to pitch in and what role you should play. Sometimes you will need to take on different roles to get things done. To get all of us out of the pit, we each had to assume different roles at different times. Sometimes I helped to push and to be leverage for another person. At other times, I lay on my belly, pulling someone out of the pit.

Learn to be flexible in a team environment, how to do other tasks within the team, and when to jump in to provide help, even if that is typically not your role. We all need to assume the role of the pinch hitter sometimes. Being flexible and being there for your teams in life and business is more valuable than you can imagine. No one likes to hear, "Well, that is not my job," or my kiddos' favorites, "It's his turn to do the dishes," or "She is supposed to clean the kitty litter box" when the reason you are asking is that the job must get done! Please, someone, jump in and help! You may not get recognized for the specific task you helped with, but people will remember you as someone who is there when needed. Believe me, in either of those two scenarios, others will note your actions.

Help Without Judgment

I want to take you through one more scenario from the Conquer the Gauntlet obstacle course race we did with our children. This one teaches us about jumping in and helping others without judging another person's ability or skill. The Belly of the Beast is difficult to explain, so I will do my best here. This obstacle requires the participant to walk up a sixteen-foot, four-inch-wide beam from about two feet off the ground to a platform that is eight feet off the ground. From there, you need to crawl under a net, not on top of it but under this net, to the ground on the other side, kicking the cowbell at the end to signify your accomplishment.

As we were waiting in line to take on this obstacle, I noticed a woman in front of us, who was attempting to walk up the balance beam, get stuck about halfway up and panic a little. She really wanted to turn around and go back down but didn't know how to do so. Another woman noticed the same thing that I did, and we both went to the stranded woman on the balance beam. We offered our hands and shoulders for the woman to balance herself on, which allowed her to turn around so she could walk back down the beam. We held her hands as she did so and got her safely to the ground. She thanked us, seeming a bit embarrassed that she had panicked. We both nodded, smiled, and said it was not a big deal at all, encouraging her by telling her that not all obstacles need to be conquered. Remember the Pegatron obstacle in Chapter 5?

As I joined my daughter back in line, she asked me what had happened. I told her that the woman didn't feel comfortable walking up the balance beam, that it made her too nervous, and that she wanted to turn around and get off of it but didn't know how. My daughter cocked her head to the side, wrinkled her nose a bit, and said, "Well, it doesn't look that difficult. Why'd she panic?" My response was that everyone faces challenges differently. What might come easy to us could be difficult for others and vice versa. It is not our place to judge but to understand that we all have strengths in different areas of our lives. If we were all the same, the world would be a very boring place.

That was another great lesson from these courses that I am so thankful to share with my kids, and one I hope they remember as they take on other challenges in life and notice that others might not be doing the same or as well as they are, or they might not be doing as well as someone else. I want them to understand that we all have different capabilities and specific strengths and weaknesses. I like to think of all of us as puzzle pieces in life. If we all were the same and could do the same things, basically had the same shaped puzzle piece, then the picture would never come together quite right. We are all different, and our differences fit together and complement each other. If someone cannot do the things that come easy to you, that is alright because I bet they can do something that doesn't come easy to you. That is a lesson we should all remember.

This also brings up the comparison demon that we discussed in Chapter 7 and Chapter 11. Try not to compare your abilities to others or others' abilities to yours. There are many things I am good at but more things I am not. For example, I could never do splits. I would like to, but I am not flexible enough to do so, and I do not care enough to put in the effort to see if I could eventually do them. I am pretty certain my body is not supposed to do splits anyway! Should others who can do them judge me? Should I be embarrassed and think less of myself because I cannot do them? Absolutely not on both accounts. I know this is a silly example, but when we compare ourselves to what others are capable of, you might as well be using the same analogy.

We are all different and excel or fail at different things. That is a good thing! We need to accept that and be the best at what we can do, and to hell with what others think and to whether or not we can keep up with them. It is your life. Live it as best you can, and let others do the same.

LESSONS FROM THE OBSTACLE COURSE

LITTLE ACTS OF KINDNESS MATTER

One other lesson from this obstacle: often in life, you can do small things to help others. You may get some words of thanks, a smile of appreciation, or a wave of the hand, and on rare occasions, you get nothing in return for your help. It shouldn't matter whether or not anyone acknowledges you for your help. Although, I will admit it is nice to get a little affirmative nod, but that shouldn't be the reason to help a stranger or a family member. We should simply help when and where we can. It is also a fun exercise to keep an eye out for ways that you can help a stranger.

What do I mean by that? Let me provide the following scenario: I would consider my height a little above average for a woman at about five foot six inches. I am at least tall enough to reach the top of a grocery shelf, just not the very top. There have been many times when I have been in the grocery store and have gotten something from the top shelf for someone in the aisle. Even when I am in a hurry to get my stuff and get out of the store, I try to keep aware of my surroundings and offer help if it seems someone needs it. I do this partly for selfish reasons because it warms my heart to help others if I can. The small task of reaching the top shelf to get something is such a minor inconvenience to me. I would do it anytime someone needed it, even if I were in a hurry.

Now I don't go around bothering people and assuming they need help—that would just be weird. But I also won't walk away or ignore an obvious situation when someone is staring at the top shelf, wondering how to get something down. Just like I do not ignore the person coming in the door behind me in a building; I hold the door open behind me so they do not have to reopen it. It is the nice thing to do. That is one important thing that these courses teach us, but sometimes I think we are missing in society as a whole.

We all signed up for this

In these races, we are all in it together. We are all going through the same obstacles. Even if we must complete many of them separately, we are still together. We are facing many similar challenges and must tackle many similar obstacles in our lives as well. It comes naturally for most of the participants in these races to stop and help another participant. It should be that way in life too. We shouldn't forget that we are all in this crazy life together.

Now I know we all face individual challenges and burdens, but even knowing that, we have many similar ones, such as paying bills, working, grocery shopping, raising children, dealing with family dynamics, and many other things. Sometimes a caring smile from a stranger can make all the difference in how a day is going.

I am not saying you must stop what you are doing and help everyone you see. But please remember, you are on this rock with a lot of other people. And even though you are going through your own obstacles, try not to forget that others are going through their own obstacles as well. If it makes sense to you to lend a hand to someone facing a similar challenge, then it might be helpful to find a group of people going through similar challenges. If that is not something you are comfortable with, then don't forget that small things make a difference. Holding a door for someone, allowing someone in on the highway, being nice to the store clerk as they check out your purchases, or even giving someone a smile can make a difference in how the day goes for both of you.

We can say the same for our business lives as well. I have been in sales for most of my career, and I can tell you that I was usually more successful at bringing on a new client when I had a teammate with me to present our services. This was especially true when it was a teammate with whom we had mutual respect and an appreciation for what the other brought to the table as we presented our services. Finding that great working relationship, regardless of whether or not you are in sales, can make all the difference in the world.

If you are working on a project for your company and you have a teammate you can count on, it makes you more successful in completing the project. To achieve such success, you need to have an appreciation and respect for each other. That includes jumping in to help each other, taking on different roles, pinch-hitting when needed, being accountable to each other, the project, or the sale, and knowing that each of you will do your part to get the job done.

Trust in your teammates

Building trust is also key to making the team successful. Thinking back to those walls and the people who provided a foothold to my daughter, a stranger, and myself, I realize we had to trust that they would not drop us and would stay steady as we reached for the top of the wall and pulled ourselves over. If they did drop us before we were ready, then we could hurt ourselves or not make it over the wall. The person creating the foothold could get hurt as well if we fell on them or maybe kicked them as we reached for the top and swung ourselves over. The same applied to climbing out of the mud pit. We had to trust that the two people pulling us from the top were going to keep a good hold on us until we got to where we could finish the climb on our own.

In business and in life, we expect the same trust from teammates in completing a project or making a sale. We know we are better when we work together and must trust that each of us will do our part. Not only are we accountable to each other, but we also create a synergy that can come when we work together. Each one of us does our part so the team accomplishes its task. This is sometimes harder to do in business than it is on those muddy fields because not everyone sees collaboration at work through a similar lens. However, if you can find those individuals whom you work well with, who you trust, who you know will do their part, and who will turn around and lend a hand so the team can be successful, then you know you have found a winning mix.

Such collaboration can be encouraged through team-building exercises or other trainings that focus on how working as a team on certain projects will make everyone successful. If fostering teamwork is important to your business, then it is worth the time to not only put these exercises together but also to explain why it is important to the overall goal of the team. Then have the team explain their experiences with working as a team once the activity is done and how that can apply to business.

It serves as a reminder for everyone that, as an individual, you can only go so far, but as a team, you can be unstoppable.

Lesson

- Don't be shy about helping others
- Identify when it is imperative that you work as a team
- Build trust in your team and yourself

Take Action

Take some time to think about how teamwork affects your personal and professional life. Where in your business or your personal life do you need to facilitate better teamwork? What part can you play to help encourage or maybe set the example of the teamwork you would like to see? As a parent, what could you model for your children that will help them see the benefits of teamwork? As a co-worker, where can you jump in to help the team you are working with? Where have you fallen short in helping your teammates? What could you do differently? As a leader, what can you do to not only demonstrate teamwork and collaboration but also where can you encourage it? Where do you discourage it?

Questions to Ponder

- When did a teamwork exercise go well? What could you repeat?
- When did it fall apart? What happened?
- What does collaboration mean to you?
- What areas of your life could you be more observant so you can help others?
- What areas of your life do you need more patience and understanding of others' abilities?
- What expectations do you have for yourself? For your family? For your co-workers? For your employees?
- Are they reasonable? Achievable?

Now that you have made it through all five of the strategies and the lessons these obstacle courses teach you, what happens after the race? Is that it? Not by a long shot! This is just the beginning.

FINALE
AFTER THE RACE

16

THE BLING

WHY DO WE RACE?

Part of the journey is the end.

—Tony Stark, *Iron Man*

One of the first things I look for when signing up for a race, whether it is a 5 km, 10 km, half-marathon, or obstacle course race, is whether the race provides a medal to those who finish. This might sound a little trivial, but I will not sign up for a race unless I get that shiny medal at the end. Well, almost never. There has been a race or two that didn't have a medal, but that is the exception, not the norm.

Maybe you can relate, but I really do like getting that shiny medal at the end of the race. To me, it is the final capstone to a long process, the months of training and putting in the reps, regardless of whether I felt like doing them. It is something to hang on my wall to remind me of my accomplishment, not only on that day but also of the months of training leading up to race day.

Like many other participants, I have a place on my wall to hang all those medals, so I see them every day when I walk out of my bedroom. It reminds me of what I have accomplished over the years, the challenges I have faced, and all the fun we had on those days with family and friends, both those that came with us and those that we met on the course. Also, it inspires me to keep up the good fight and continue to pursue more medals to hang on the wall. Which helps keep me motivated to stick with my workout routine, nutrition plan, and, let's be honest, it keeps me feeling young!

So what is in it for you? Why do you race? Why do you take on challenges in your life? Or why don't you?

We have so many reasons we choose to race, whether it is to complete your first race or one-hundredth. The feeling of accomplishment once you cross that finish line reminds you to celebrate the big wins you have in life. But it isn't just the big ones that we need to celebrate; it is also the little milestones we met along the way to get to the big win.

Maybe it was when you could increase the distance on your run, lift more weight than you did a month ago, or do more push-ups or pull-ups (still a struggle for me!). Whatever it was, celebrate those small milestones you met along the way too. While you have no medals to hang on your wall for those, you can recognize those little wins so that each one will propel you forward. And studies show that you need to!

STOP AND SMELL THE ROSES

Here's the thing: if we lived only for the big wins that put bling on our walls, we would miss out on the little wins and accomplishments we have made along the way. The little wins push us forward, make our day, and give us a reason to continue to push toward the big one. Much like I mentioned on that big hill in Chapter 7, each step you take can be a win. It's not to say you have a big celebration at each one—that defeats the purpose because you lose the effect of celebrating the finale. However, reaching milestones that are part of your training program, or part of a project, allows you to take a break to see how far you have come. Recognize it, applaud it, then take a deep breath and start working toward the next milestone.

Recent studies also suggest a little dopamine action goes on that can help encourage us to keep moving forward and is why it might be important to do a little celebratory dance when you reach a milestone. The feel-good sensation that dopamine gives can act as a motivating factor to push you onward and upward to meet your next milestone and the overall end goal of a race or project. But much like the overuse of anything, don't overdo it. Don't make too many milestone celebrations, as the effect of that dopamine injection can fade and lose its impact on your psyche.

So how does this relate to the bling at the end of races, and how can you use this to motivate you in your life and business? Well, when you take the time to recognize your accomplishments, you can create the same effect on your brain and your confidence. The simple act of marking the end of a long trial has a tremendous impact on your psyche. Since our brains crave that reward, why not use it to your advantage? Boost your confidence and those feel-good endorphins by celebrating your accomplishments, not just at the end of an extensive project but at milestones along the way as you pursue your goals.

Forget the Pain

That dopamine release does another thing that those who have ever given birth can attest to. Much like being handed that new bundle of joy after what could have been hours of agony, dopamine helps you to forget all the pain, misery, and suffering you have gone through, not only on the day of the big event but in the months leading up to it. The ability to forget, or at least minimize, the months of training and the trials of the day are all washed away when they place the medal around your neck. That is why so many of us have big, beaming smiles as we cross that finish line, rejoicing in the accomplishment of the day and the months before. And why we are so quick to sign up for another race and to continue to challenge ourselves. We simply forgot how painful the whole experience was! Which means you are not only a glutton for punishment, but you also thought the entire agonizing experience was fun! And it is. Just like giving birth, the pain mixed with a tremendous sense of accomplishment is well worth the experience and worth going for again.

What all of this leads to is that we faced our demons, our fears, our failures, and our successes, and we finished the race. We put in the hard work, overcame, and conquered! When we do this, our confidence increases, and our sense of pride in ourselves and our teammates, family, friends, or whoever joined us on the course or obstacle we faced swells. This confidence propels us forward to accomplish new things and even harder things. It also makes us look back and realize that maybe the obstacle wasn't as bad as we had made it out to be, and if you had to face it again, you could do so. It is that sense of relief you feel when something hard is over, and you do not have to do it ever again: if you choose not to. You came, you saw, you conquered, and now you are done, never to face it again. And that is okay too!

Every time we challenge ourselves, push ourselves, we get stronger—in mind, body, and spirit. That is part of the reason for doing these races repeatedly. I keep going back because I never want to forget that I can do the hard things and that I should do the hard things, no matter how old I get, and that each time I face a challenge, I get stronger. We also keep going back because I never want to get too comfortable in life. The challenges keep us young and sharp. They propel us forward to keep reaching new heights and keep us from getting fat and lazy on the couch! It works for that too!

Whatever your reason for doing the hard things in life, in business, or on those muddy fields, make sure you are doing them for your reasons, not someone else's. You will get more out of the experience, and that bling you get at the end will have much more meaning for you.

Pulling it all together

Through the lens of these obstacle courses, I have taken you through the five strategies we use as we move through challenges or obstacles in our lives: Recovery, Discovery, Persistency, Creativity, and Collaboration. With each strategy, we went through the mental and physical challenges we faced. We also discussed that how we tackled these obstacles could be applied to how we take on challenges we face in life.

We may not use these strategies in the exact order I presented them here, and we will revisit certain strategies continuously throughout our lives. But the challenges are similar, and our struggles are real. So when you feel particularly challenged in one area, go back through that section and reach for inspiration to help pull you through or maybe find that little nugget you need to overcome the challenge at hand. To help you find which chapter to lean on, here is a recap of the five strategies.

Recovery

In Recovery, we discussed how we are all healing from something, whether it is an injury, illness, false or stagnating belief about ourselves, overwork, unhappiness, frustration, lack of motivation, or something else. You name it; we are all recovering from something. To recover, though, you need a plan, a goal or something to fight for, and a reason to recover. You need to understand your limitations, what you can do now, what you must work with, and what you need to work on. You also must be able to acknowledge when you need to pass and come back to fight another day or not at all. Whatever approach or decision you make, you need to be okay with it, accept it, rejoice in your accomplishments, and move on to fight another day or battle.

Discovery

In Discovery, we highlighted that sometimes you need to find your purpose in order to overcome certain challenges in your life. To understand why you need to take on the challenge in the first place or why maybe it is not worth the fight at all. When you understand what your purpose is in facing a certain challenge, why you need to get through it or over it, and what benefit it provides you, you are better equipped to take it on. To do so, you may need to ask yourself several questions, identify your excuses (what is holding you back), and decide if it is worth it to fight or better to walk away.

Persistency

In Persistency, we learned that sometimes things in life are not that easy, but they are doable. When you understand what you are recovering from and you have decided that it is worth taking on the challenge, now is the time to fight the good fight! What does it take to hang in there? And what efforts do you need to put forth? Do you need training or preparation, and if so, what kind? How strong is your reason for pushing through, and what do you do when you want to give up? Preparation is the key to success, but so is continual self-evaluation and returning to your reason for wanting to take on the challenge in the first place. Being able to evaluate why you want to make the change or take on a challenge helps you get through the moments when you want to quit. Also, your answer might provide you with the pure gut persistence to push through to make it happen despite all the challenges you are facing.

CREATIVITY

In Creativity, we recognized that not all things in life are straightforward. Sometimes, to accomplish the goal, you need to tap into your imagination and think outside the box. But when you are in the thick of it, it's difficult to pull yourself out to see the entire forest. Learning to take a pause, even when you think you can't, will save you a lot of hurt, frustration, and failure. It is also important to recognize that someone might be watching to see how you do things, not to criticize but to learn. Your actions might make a difference for someone else who is going through the same obstacles that you are. Identify when taking the time to think can make all the difference in whether or not you will succeed at the task at hand. But remember, being creative doesn't mean perfection, either. Sometimes it only means getting the job done.

COLLABORATION

Last is Collaboration. You understand that it is important to acknowledge that you cannot do everything by yourself, and on some obstacles or challenges, you will need help. What can be difficult for many is identifying not only when you need help but also taking aid when others offer it and helping others when needed. You also identified who your Rock is and who you are the Rock for, and why it is so important to have this person in your life and to be this person for someone else. On the obstacle course, it comes naturally to help others in need and to receive help when you need it. Taking this approach to life can assist you in identifying when it might be good to step in to offer your help to others, when it could be beneficial to ask for help yourself, and why we need each other to overcome an obstacle when life gets challenging.

Life is nothing but a huge obstacle course to manage through, or maybe it is like several of them. Each time you pass a milestone, you get a little celebratory bling, then you move on to the next. It's like each birthday or New Year when you get to hit the reset button and play again. Don't forget to go out there and play, though, no matter how old you are. Take on new challenges and push yourself to be better today than you were yesterday.

Now's the time to jump in and get dirty!

I look forward to seeing you out on those muddy fields of life!

ACKNOWLEDGMENTS

A big thank you goes out to my family, Frank, Gavin, and Tori—for not only supporting me in this endeavor but cheering me on, keeping me accountable, and being my inspiration. You make me want to strive to be the best mother and wife I can be. Love you all tons!

To Carol Anne Taylor for your support and encouragement. Our meetings helped keep me on task and moving forward. I am thankful to have randomly met you and that you have become a part of this journey with me.

For the ladies who I have met through the ADAPT Functional Health Coach program, Pam Griswold, Beth Farleigh, Desiree Yanez, Allison Shore, Amy Brandley, and Tatiana Vertucci. I am extremely fortunate to have met you and greatly appreciate your support and encouragement, not just through our Health Coaching certification program, but also for the life support through these crazy past two years.

To Daphne Smith for encouraging me to step out and to take a chance and be a wave-maker! You lead by example in all things you do. Your energy and enthusiasm are contagious. So glad we met all those years ago!

To my extended family and friends for not laughing when I told them I was writing a book. I appreciate the check-ins, encouragement, and support, even if you thought I was crazy!

I definitely need to acknowledge the Arvest Crew who introduced me to these races and for being a part of the fun in that first race back in 2014. Thank you for inviting me and for introducing me to this world of obstacle course challenges! I am forever grateful! Barbara Mills, Janet Wedman, Diane Wells, and Calvin Jarod & family.

To Jayme Boston for listening to me walk through my ideas on our many runs. I miss those! Your patience and encouragement have been a tremendous help along this path.

For my book readers—Carol Anne Taylor, Dawn Walker, Liz Lucus, and Jayme Boston. Your feedback was invaluable. I appreciate the time you took to review and comment. I took all to heart and did my best to incorporate all your great suggestions.

This section would not be complete if I didn't acknowledge the makers of these great obstacle course challenges—especially the ones I have participated in so far! To the creators & all the volunteers of the Conquer the Gauntlet OCR—Mainprize Industries, LLC (David, Steve, and Courtney). Thank you for putting these challenges together. I can only imagine the hard work and dedication it takes to put on these races each year. I am so glad you do and hope that this tradition continues for years to come. I plan on being out there each year, and I have many more years to go!!

For the Spartan and Tough Mudder series under the umbrella of Joe DeSena's Spartan Race, Inc. the most well-known of the obstacle course challenges. These were the races we aimed for as we got to know more about these challenges. There are so many more for us to take on, and we are looking forward to tackling them in future years.

The Warrior Dash was the one that started it all for us. Sadly, it is not in operation anymore. We are so thankful for those first races we took on with our friends and our kids, though. It was the festive environment and the fun of the challenges that got us hooked on these races. I understand that all good things come to an end at some point, but this race series will always hold a special place in my heart and our lives.

My final acknowledgment goes out to my dear friend Sandi Moninger who we lost in 2015. My heart still aches, but you will always be a part of our family and me. Miss you much, friend!

~Kelly

ENDNOTES

1. Conquer The Gauntlet. https://www.conquerthegauntlet.com/
2. *Galaxy Quest*. Directed by Dean Parisot. 1999. Universal City, California: DreamWorks SKG, 2000. DVD.
3. Stulberg, Brad, and Steve Magness. *Peak Performance: Elevate Your Game, Avoid Burnout, and Thrive with the New Science of Success*. Pennsylvania: Rodale Books, 2017.
4. Mayo Clinic Staff. "Stress relief from laughter? It's no joke." *Mayo Clinic*. Last modified July 29, 2021. https://www.mayoclinic.org/healthy-lifestyle/stress-management/in-depth/stress-relief/art-20044456.
5. Lawrence Robinson, Melinda Smith, M.A., and Jeanne Segal, Ph.D. "Laughter is the Best Medicine." *HelpGuide*. Last updated July 2021. https://www.helpguide.org/articles/mental-health/laughter-is-the-best-medicine.htm.

Power Through Wellness
Coaching

Author | Speaker | Workshop Facilitator

Kelly knows the importance of choosing a speaker who will meet your needs. One who will be engaging and will leave the audience with valuable information they are able to implement immediately.

Her easygoing and dynamic style makes her a great fit for any conference, workshop, or event.

For more information, contact Kelly at:

www.kellymajdan.com
kelly@kellymajdan.com

Power Through Wellness
Coaching

Design Your Wellness Strategy

CLARIFY
Your wellness objectives to know where to invest your time, money, and resources

IDENTIFY
What you enjoy to make it easier to integrate healthy habits into your life.

ACT
Choose one step to act on in 90 days to move you closer to living a life of health and longevity.

"Planning is bringing the future into the present so that you can do something about it now."

—Alan Lakein

Connect with Kelly to learn more about **Design Your Wellness Strategy**© and other programs, workshops, and speaking engagements at www.kellymajdan.com.

Powered by Easy IP™

www.ingramcontent.com/pod-product-compliance
Lightning Source LLC
Chambersburg PA
CBHW071239070526
44583CB00017B/2246